FULLY ENGAGED

FULLY ENGAGED

Shift from Average
to AWESOME in 46 Days

ADAIR CATES

Fully Engaged: Shift from Average to Awesome in 46 Days

Copyright © 2014 by Adair Cates.

All Rights Reserved. No part of this book may be reproduced, transmitted, or stored in any form or by any means whatsoever without express written permission in advance from the author, except in brief quotations in critical articles or reviews.

www.adaircates.com

First printing 2014
ISBN: 978-0-9915127-0-6

Cover and interior design by Adina Cucicov, Flamingo Designs.
Cover image © Denys Rudyi - Fotolia.com

Dedication

I thank the village of wonderful souls who surround me for showing me how to live their version of a meaning-full life. Thank you, Chris, for loving all sides of me, even the ones you're not too crazy about, and for inspiring creativity in me. Thank you, Mozart, Ringo, and Wario, for being my furry babies who teach me unconditional love in every moment. Thank you, Mom and Dad, for bringing me up to be so well-rounded and encouraging me to try different things. Thanks to my sister for being my forever and constant friend. Thanks to all of my special friends and family (too many to acknowledge individually) who bring so much joy and meaning to my life. You are SO loved!

I also want to acknowledge myself, for stepping out and writing another book after five years. Thank you, me, for being more candid and honest in this one, for speaking my truth authentically even when I knew that it wouldn't please everyone. Thank you, me, for standing on the ledge of my comfort zone and being my most vulnerable self, all for the sake of living a fully engaged life.

Table of Contents

Preface 1
This Book is for ME and for YOU 5
How to Experience This Book 9
Day 1: Perfectly Imperfect 13
Day 2: Peeling an Onion Will Make You Cry 17
Day 3: From Tension to Intention 21
Day 4: Thinking of Fans Instead of Critics 25
Day 5: Risk Criticism or Face Mediocrity 29
Day 6: You Are More Than Your Circumstances 33
Day 7: Freedom vs. Discipline 37
Day 8: Is Compassion Overrated? 43
Day 9: Your I AM Super Power 47
Day 10: Affirming You're Awesome 51
Day 11: Putting a Fence Up Around Your Life 55
Day 12: No More Either/Or. Instead, I'll Have Both 59
Day 13: Write Your Life 63
Day 14: 60,000 – 50,000 – 80 – 95 69
Day 15: Being "Normal" Sucks! 73
Day 16: There's No Such Thing as Small Change 77
Day 17: Henry Ford Jacked Us All Up 81
Day 18: Picking Yourself 85
Day 19: Steamy Desire 89
Day 20: Living in a Material World Is SOOOOO Eighties ... 93

Day 21: Ditch the Pursuit of Perfection ... 97
Day 22: Being Grateful "As Is" ... 101
Day 23: The World Behind the World ... 105
Day 24: Brain Connections ... 109
Day 25: Action to Create New Habits ... 113
Day 26: Why Practice for Seven Hours When You Can Visualize for One? ... 117
Day 27: Subconsciously Rewiring Your Thoughts ... 121
Day 28: Give People Their S@%* Back (figuratively and literally) ... 125
Day 29: Control + Alt + Delete ... 129
Day 30: Stop Slouching! Stand Up and Be Proud to Be You! ... 133
Day 31: Everyone is Busy, So Stop Saying That! ... 137
Day 32: Tame is (Mostly) Lame ... 141
Day 33: Misery is Optional ... 145
Day 34: Too Big for Your Britches ... 149
Day 35: The Habit of Living on the Surface ... 153
Day 36: Go for It! ... 157
Day 37: Clarity = Power ... 161
Day 38: Your Ten Objects ... 165
Day 39: What Do You Value? ... 169
Day 40: My Personal Credo ... 173
Day 41: Bark with Passion! ... 177
Day 42: Falling in Love with ME! ... 181
Day 43: Be Willing to Receive ... 185
Day 44: Practice DOES NOT Makes Perfect ... 189
Day 45: Growth Can Be Uncomfortable ... 193
Day 46: This Is Going to Sound Morbid, But Don't Skip This! ... 197
Conclusion ... 201

Preface

Imagine you're at the most important soccer game of the year or a basketball game being played by two teams with a longstanding and fierce rivalry (think Carolina v. Duke). The crowds scream and cheer and can't contain their passion and excitement. Now, imagine getting this excited about things that are really meaningful. About your life, your goals, even your daily experiences. What if you could live your life in ways that fulfill you instead of doing things that just help you pass the time, like playing CandyCrush? Don't get me wrong—distractions are fun, and important on occasion, but we're surrounded by them, and they have a way of consuming us. Too many of us conduct our lives as if the whole thing was one big distraction. We make so many choices without reflecting on our purpose. We pass up so many opportunities to have joyful, fulfilled, lives. We are missing out on living the best lives that we possibly can.

I've been aware of this for a long time. In many ways I was a typical teen—I had a poster of each New Kid on the Block and magazine snippets of cool gear I wanted on my walls. I had a stuffed animal hammock overflowing in the corner... but I also had a serious, reflective side. Amongst my collage of wall decor, I hung my favorite quote, printed from my dot matrix printer, "The purpose of life is a life of purpose." I knew deep inside that meaning mattered. I wanted to have different experiences, meet all kinds of people, take chances, try things. I don't mean that I wanted to take particularly dangerous chances or try really risky things—except, of course, that every time you try something new there's risk in it, and new things might always feel somewhat dangerous. But even as a youngster I intentionally set my mind to taking the risks of learning new things.

In college I had an experience—well, actually several experiences, but I'm only going to talk about one here—that changed my life. I studied abroad in Sevilla, Spain, for a year to totally immerse myself in the language and the culture. Living among Spaniards rather than among Americans was thrilling—to be so responsible for myself, especially before I really learned the language well, to have no choice but to go out on a limb every day and open myself up to so much that was new.

It was an incredible experience, and after graduation I returned there to teach English and met a woman (whom you'll read about later) who really opened my eyes to the kinds of power that each one of us has over our own lives. She helped me shape my life's philosophies. One thing became very clear to me then: we each have the power to shift our own reality. That power is rooted in the mind. (The mind, of course, is inextricably bound up with the physical body. This book is much more about mind than body, but suffice it to say that your physical body is an imprint of what's going on in your head, your brain, your mind. More about that in my next book.)

After my time in Spain, I moved on to teaching school and taught kids of all ages for eight years. Not only did I teach them the subject matter I specialized in (which was Spanish, naturally), but I also worked with them on how to "show up" in their own lives—really, how to live authentically and find meaning.

But something was missing from teaching. I wanted something more. That's when I decided to take a leap of faith, quit my job, write my first book and go out on my own as a speaker and trainer. That was a fun but tough year with lots of important lessons (don't jump before you're ready!). It wasn't long before my plan failed, I ran out of money and was back to teaching Spanish at my childhood rival high school, driving an hour each way. Challenging to say the least. But somehow I made the best of it. In fact, in 2010, I wrote a blog post each day about intentionally choosing to feel good even when circumstances are not ideal. By the end of that year, I had a new job that I loved (my first corporate job!) and Chris and I moved to Atlanta where we reside today.

Now that I've moved into the corporate world, I'm fortunate to train and coach adults of all ages to live up to their potential and find meaning in their work and life. I get to do work I love and to share my message every day. For my "students" of all ages, it's always been absolutely clear to me that the way people can best modify their behaviors in ways that are beneficial—and in ways that will last—is to first change their thinking.

I owe debts of gratitude to many people, particularly Wayne Dyer, Jack Canfield, Bob Proctor, and Rhonda Byrne. The things that I've learned from them (and many other teachers you'll hear about in the book) have been transformative for me. As I've synthesized all the things I've learned in life so far, I've got some new ideas and techniques to offer you as you seek to become your own perfectly imperfect, fully realized self. With some motivation, following some simple prescriptions, and a good dose of god juju (read on!), you're on your way.

I look forward to accompanying you on this journey to a fully engaged life.

Adair Cates
January 2014

This Book is for ME and for YOU

This book was born at the corner of my sweet Southern people-pleaser self and my bold and free spirited soul, at the juncture of the me that cares waaaaaayyyyy too much what everybody else thinks and the me who chooses the road less traveled. It's appropriate for you to know that I'm a Pisces, so two fish swimming in opposite directions—my astrological sign—may help explain the two me's that live in here.

In truth, I'm just like many women who hide their true selves quite often because it's safe and it feels like the right thing to do. If everything looks perfect on the outside, then I must be perfect on the inside too. Right?

I *never* did this as a child (and I'll bet you didn't either). But somehow when I hit about twenty-five, all of that changed (hence my belief that the quarter-life crisis is real). I was an "adult" and it was time to *act* like an adult. That's when my mini-anxiety attacks and dizzy spells started too. Is there a correlation? Probably. Because hiding behind this person that the world wants me to be is a fabulous free-spirited soul with a lot to say and offer. The feeling when not allowed to be the real ME is dizzying, and keeping that spirit concealed feels blasphemous. So why do I do it? Why do you do it? I hope this book can help us both know why. And more than that—it will help us STOP being someone other than our true, authentic selves. (At least most of the time).

The world teaches us that in order to fit in, we have to fly under the radar, not ruffle any feathers, and do what others tell us to do. In the process of trying to get it all right, we lose our own sense of purpose and meaning. But is that what we really want—"to fit in"? Or is our purpose to be something more?

It reminds me of the story of the velveteen rabbit. Did you ever read that book? The humble velveteen rabbit lives with many other more expensive mechanical toys, like metal wind-up soldiers and stately wooden lions. He feels quite insignificant among the modern toys until he meets the skin horse who reminds him that being "real" isn't about how you're made, but about opening up to love and accepting your uniqueness. The skin horse tells the velveteen rabbit that being real might mean having your skin rubbed off and your eyes scratched. Though the velveteen rabbit longed to be real, he wished that he could become it without these uncomfortable things happening to him. "It doesn't happen all at once," the skin horse told the velveteen rabbit. "You become. It takes a long time. That's why it doesn't happen often to people who break easily, or have sharp edges, or who have to be carefully kept."

The same goes for you. To live a meaningful life, you have to be ok with imperfection and discomfort. Many of us act like the mechanical toys: uniform in the way we conform to certain ideals, adhering to what's expected of us. When what we all want more than anything is to let our hair down and be who we really are, be real, even if the world disapproves. To be real is to live a life of meaning. It means being perfectly imperfect. It's realizing that life is too short to be a mechanical toy.

I can't tell you how many books I've wanted to write since writing and self-publishing my first, over five years ago. I've had all kinds of great ideas, but none of them were *originally* mine—most were a recycled version of what another self-help author/motivational speaker had to say. In the world of *The Velveteen Rabbit*, my "modern ideas" would have been understood as what *the world* wanted me to say, not what *I* really wanted to say.

Don't get me wrong, these self-help authors and motivational speakers are my heroes and have made a lasting impact on me. But at the end of the day, I realized that finding myself through the messages of others, focusing outward instead of inward, can make me lose who I really am. Always wanting to improve myself through just one more three-step process makes me feel like I'm not already good enough—when I know that essentially I am. Thus, the birth of this book. This isn't meant to be a "self-help" book, in the sense that I won't tell you how to make more friends, make more money, or cure your nail-biting habit. Instead, it's rather an exploratory guide of your own being-ness. My hope is that through this book you will come to understand how much more beautiful and real life is when your edges are worn off.

My hope is that you read something in this book that you can relate to, and breathe a sigh of relief at knowing that you're not crazy, not the only one who has ridiculous thoughts, not the only one with big questions about life. The intention of this book, as I share stories and ideas, is, most importantly, to ask you questions that will get you thinking and acting in ways that give you the opportunity to be fully engaged in your life. The format of the book is intended to spur thought and then action, so get your pen out and be ready to represent. After each section, the questions you'll ponder will lead to actions to take. Are you ready to begin this journey with me? Let's get started!

How to Experience This Book

You need:

- A journal (in case you run out of space in the book)
- Your favorite writing instrument and
- 15-20 minutes every day for the next forty-six days

To get the most benefit out of this book, and more importantly, to get closer to living a more fully engaged life, you have to make a commitment to read one passage per day *and* follow along with the questions to ponder, thoughts to think, and actions to take.

When you fully engage with this book, you'll see that you'll be more fully engaged with your life. Before you get there, though, you have some territory to cross. The first barrier that you'll probably encounter is the excuse that you don't have enough time. But you know, if people spent as much time finding meaning and joy in their lives as they do playing CandyCrush and Farmville or PS4, our world would look *way* different. All I'm asking for is 15–20 minutes of your day. I promise you this: you're not going be on your deathbed regretting not having played enough online games. Disconnect from that crap and re-connect with yourself. The real "joystick" in life is navigating with passion and purpose.

You may ask why I didn't make this a 365-day guide. Well, knowing the short attention span most of us have (me included!), a month and a half is sufficient to get you on the road—it's a good way to get into gear.

At first this may not feel comfortable—change is often tough for people. On your journey to becoming more fully engaged in your life, you'll hit some bumps in the road, and you may even have a flat tire or a breakdown. Just like any new habit, be aware that you'll be most unsure and likely to give up during the first days you practice. But with this, keep in mind, if you're not uncomfortable, you're not learning. As I often say, *we have to live with tension to live with intention.*

Also, you may find some of the passages in the book slightly overlap one other. Focus on the passage for the day and if you come to a passage that confuses your earlier learning, see if you can find the balance that's closest to perfect for you. Living an engaged and meaningful life requires a healthy tension between two often distant ends of a spectrum. I don't know what the perfectly imperfect balance is for you. And you may not either at this point. I hope this book helps you find out.

How to Experience This Book

Pondering the questions I've provided is an opportunity for you to explore what you think and feel. The "thought to think" is your daily affirmation/mantra, good to repeat in your head when the gremlin starts grumbling, while you're in savasana in yoga class, or in a traffic jam about to pull your hair out. The action for the day might be the most important piece of the whole equation. A whole lot of people like to buy books—and about 95 percent of those books never get read. So if you've gotten this far, you're already winning. A whole lot fewer people actually change their behavior based on something they read. The winners of the world are the readers and doers. You've got to act more engaged to BE more engaged.

I know that you are dedicated to seeing this through (because, hell, you've gotten this far, you can see the purpose!). Of course, at first, just like when you start any new routine, you're going to find it challenging to commit. You may skip a day here and there; you may get frustrated; you may feel like giving up. But keep on pushing, even if you start and stop more than once. Or don't keep on pushing—and keep living your mediocre, blah, life. But that's not what you want, is it? You're in charge, and this is your opportunity to get on that path to making your life all that it can be. The journey of a thousand miles begins with a single step.

DAY 1

Perfectly Imperfect

6/30/15

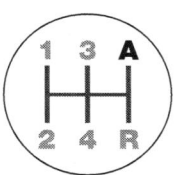

"Perfect imperfection is a beautiful sight to behold. In fact, it can change the way you look at life...if you simply let it."

Rachel Macy Stafford

I first used the two words "perfectly imperfect" together to describe my college BFF's new boyfriend when I first met him. After the three of us enjoyed seafood and cocktails in a swanky outdoor spot in Manhattan, she and I did a mini-escape/refresh in the bathroom, and she asked me what I thought of him. She thought he was "the one" and wanted to know my opinion. I answered, "He is perfectly imperfect." I loved him from our first meeting because of his boy-next-door good looks and unpretentious nature.

Fully Engaged

Not only did I love *him*, I also loved my new phrase. Then, over the last several years I completely forgot about it, as I tried WAY too hard to live a perfectly perfect life. As I began to let go and rediscover the beauty of imperfection, I remembered that phrase—and the idea—and I am ready to explore perfect imperfection again, but this time with you! Here's your first assignment.

Questions to ponder:

How would you describe yourself?

warm, smart, funny, loving, honest, caring, hardworking, fair, strong, trustworthy, nonjudgemental

How would others describe you?

funny, nice, hardworking, silly

Day 1: Perfectly Imperfect

How happy are you being you?

Very happy - glad with where I am with clear visions of what I can change to be better - pleaser, care a bit too much, put others first too often

Thought to Think:

I am embracing my imperfections.

Action to Take:

Watch this video about how we often see ourselves as much more imperfect than we really are: http://www.youtube.com/watch?v=litXW91UauE.

What did you think? Write down any thoughts you have.

_____
_____
_____
_____

DAY 2

Peeling an Onion Will Make You Cry

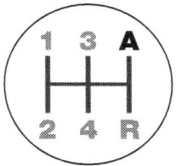

"What is necessary to change a person is to change his awareness of himself."

Abraham Maslow

We are multi-layered and faceted beings, and we often compare this phenom to an onion by saying that as we learn more and more about ourselves and have realizations and experience growth, we are peeling back layers of the onion. Be aware: peeling an onion might make you cry. So be prepared. Admitting that we have less love for ourselves than we have for anyone on the planet is sad. Thinking about this makes one of my layers want to curl up on the sofa and cry.

Fully Engaged

This journey of getting to know yourself and your sweet soul can be grueling (and pungent), but I promise it will be one of the most rewarding experiences of your life. Just as the skin horse told the velveteen rabbit: once you become real, you cannot become unreal.

Awareness is emotional. It's emotional because when you learn something new about yourself you have the choice to change it or to remain the same. Have you ever heard the maxim, "If you keep doing what you've always done, you'll keep getting what you've always gotten"?

Though we often avoid any place of discomfort to keep ourselves safe, opening up and experiencing emotions is a powerful impetus for growth and development. Sometimes you have to be at a place of pulling your hair out to finally make the shift, to pull back the layer of the onion, be vulnerable and expose the REAL you. Maybe that's what it feels like to be naked on stage.

But there is nothing to fear. If everyone were truly honest with themselves, we would have lots of layers to peel back (for the rest of our lives). It's ok to curl up on the couch for a minute to cry. But that won't change the world and that won't change you. If you're not ready to dig into yourself, though, give yourself a break and come back later.

Day 2: Peeling an Onion Will Make You Cry

 Questions to ponder:

What layer(s) have you peeled back on your life already?

> I can be alone and be OK. I am affected by my childhood and father. Being too nice will not get me where I want to be - I will lose. I have flaws/vices that may not change (procrastination, being laidback & lazy?)

What realization(s) made a big impact on the course of your life?

> Being happy may mean being alone. When I hold myself accountable, I can change. Speak your mind - say what you want & don't want and this shapes the life you want.

 Thought to Think:

The more I get to know myself, the more I love myself.

Action to Take:

Close your eyes and see yourself surrounded by great white light. Breathe. And breathe some more. Do this for five minutes. You are safe.

DAY 3

From Tension to Intention

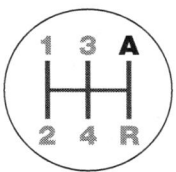

"The world is all gates, all opportunities, strings of tension waiting to be struck."

Ralph Waldo Emerson

What do you think of when you hear the word "tension"? I think of a rubber band being stretched out, a taut slingshot, a balloon on the verge of popping. I think of the tightness and discomfort in my shoulders and neck when I'm feeling stressed. I think of a room where you can cut the awkwardness in the air with a knife.

We live in a world full of tension, and we've been trained to loathe it, to judge it and ourselves when we are feeling anything less than perfect. But if we can change our view of the tension—from negative to more positive—we can use it as a jumping off point to get us from where we are to where we want to be. Some of the most tense situations in life are awesome opportunities to choose expansion, growth, and taking life to the next level.

In tension there is energy—like a slingshot being pulled back, and then being released. Whatever has been shot (an arrow, a rock, your intention!) flies through the air towards its target. And if things work out just right, it ends up on the mark.

We can do that too—use our tension as a jumping off place towards whatever goal we're aiming at. For example, look at a situation I was in last week. The company I work for is going through a re-org so people are losing their jobs, some being moved around, and some demoted. As a learning consultant in a large healthcare organization, when times get tough my job is likely not viewed as "essential." I've been in this type of re-org situation before when things did NOT turn our well for me. In this case, after many emotional conversations and accidentally divulging too much information to one group, I felt totally depleted. The tension had been too much! Then I realized that this tension is a valuable experience to have on my way toward being a leader in my field, since being a leader means having to deal with tough situations like this on a regular basis. And though I'm sure I'll never *enjoy* going through it again, I can now view

Day 3: From Tension to Intention

the tension as part of the energy to propel me forward and offer me much-needed leadership experience to be successful in the future.

Often tension is nothing more than your higher self telling you that it's ready to move on, and the resistance you feel is your ego holding you in the past. When some (or maybe most) areas of your life are making you feel tense, drained, and exhausted, the universe is trying to tell you something. Your small, habitual self wants to keep you in your little bubble of a comfort zone while the bigger, bolder, more daring version of you wants to move on to conquer new horizons. I have experienced this tension so many times. Even though I know it's just a sign of my resistance, I still judge it and myself, and I want it to go away. Keep this formula in mind: Pain + Resistance = Suffering. (You can read more about that in Kristin Neff's book *SelfCompassion*.)

Questions to Ponder:

How have you used tension positively in the past?

Opportunity to address long-seated issues. Motivator to accomplish things

Fully Engaged

Where can you use tension to propel you towards one of your goals?

Career wise, moving up; proving my ability to work under pressure, solve problems and resolve issues; motivation to finish large and/or overwhelming projects

Where are you feeling tension and discomfort in your life right now?

A bit w/ Ahmed, lots @ work - 94th Rd DB/ME vs Raymond

But I realize this always changes

Thought to Think:

I am expanding and growing from the tension in my life.

Action to Take:

Pick up a rubber band and play with it. Notice the energy it collects as you stretch it. Think about how tension can cause the same kind of energy build-up in you and how you can harness it to move out of your comfort zone and into your growth zone.

DAY 4
Thinking of Fans Instead of Critics

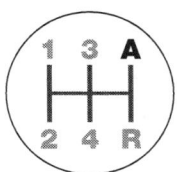

"Great spirits have always encountered violent opposition from mediocre minds."
Albert Einstein

Why is it that when we start a new endeavor we think of obstacles instead of opportunities, critics instead of fans? We ask questions like, "What could go wrong?" when really there so much more value in asking, "What could go right?" We also tend to think of the people (individually and collectively) who will not like our work or may possibly even be offended by it. Such a waste of time (and such an easy way to stay stuck in the status quo), yet we all do it! It's like having a performance review at work where the boss names ten positive things and one "opportunity for growth," and that one "developmental opportunity" is all we can focus on.

Today I had an opportunity to do a check-up from the neck up on myself. I awoke feeling excited and delighted to have a vacation day. I took full advantage of the opportunity to spend extra time enjoying my coffee and writing in my journal. As usual, I finished that writing and meditation time feeling calm, centered and confident.

During the second half of the morning I worked on sending out emails and crafting a speaking proposal.

And then it happened.

As I was putting together the speaking proposal, I came across a very unfavorable review of my book *Live with Intention* on Amazon.com. (Go ahead, read it. You know you want to.)

Let's just say after reading *that*, I felt deflated and crappy, and I wondered how I could make myself feel better. So I started by looking at other people's books to see if they'd gotten any not-so-positive reviews. And indeed they had. And I felt a little better. (I admit it. That's another way I'm not perfect. I experience a bit of *schadenfreude* from time to time, like most everyone else.)

Day 4: Thinking of Fans Instead of Critics

But I still hadn't bounced back to where I wanted to be. So I asked myself, "Is this the way a *leader* would act? Is this the way that the *strong* and *resilient* woman that I am *should* act?"

At that moment I decided that the one thing that keeps many people small in life is the exact fear I was brushing up against: the fear of criticism. Nothing significant will ever happen if we allow ourselves to be paralyzed by the fear of criticism or the fear of failure. Putting myself out there by publishing my own words in a book automatically made me vulnerable to a world of criticism. Filmmakers do it all the time. So do other authors, and cooks, and performers, and so many other people. If they can do it, so can I!

Side note: If you think that being more successful or making more money or reaching a certain level of fame will dispel this problem of looking at the one negative in a sea of positives, think again. There's a great story about Larry David, of *Seinfeld* fame. He was attending a professional sporting event in his hometown of Brooklyn and when the cameramen at the stadium saw him, they put his face on the big screen. The whole stadium erupted in cheers of celebration and homage to his awesomeness. He was shocked by the reception. But as he left the stadium feeling humbled by the experience, one raucous fan yelled at him, "Hey Larry, you suck!" Who do you think Larry David thought about for the next twenty-four hours? The tens of thousands of adoring fans, or the one jackass who yelled at him when it was all over? You got it. The jerk.

Fully Engaged

Questions to Ponder:

What fear is stopping you today?

_____
_____
_____
_____

What would you do if you knew you could not fail?

_____
_____
_____
_____

Thought to Think:

I am open only to the good opinion of others.

Action to Take:

Stop beating yourself up. If someone didn't agree with something you were doing, it was probably something risky and awesome. Forgive yourself and move on. If you're not pissing somebody off, you're probably not making enough progress. Go punch a pillow and pretend it's the critics. Scream all of your frustration into it. And keep going for it!

DAY 5
Risk Criticism or Face Mediocrity

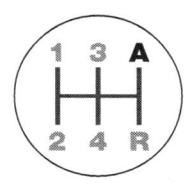

"But he'd learned long ago that a life lived without risks pretty much wasn't worth living. Life rewarded courage, even when that first step was taken neck-deep in fear."

Tamera Alexander

Sticking your neck out to finally live a meaningful life is not only going to be uncomfortable for you, but for those around you as well. Think of Larry David's critic—the one we talked about yesterday. The social rejection of not being liked feels and registers in your brain the same way that a broken leg does. In fact, one study shows that taking Tylenol when you've experienced social rejection will cure your heartache. So arm yourself with some acetaminophen and a glass of water. On your journey from here to there, there will be naysayers but they will only make you feel bad if you allow them to.

Most people run from doing anything more than mediocre because then life is easier, less emotional and less painful. Yet *so* hum-drum. Staying mediocre keeps you at the same level as everyone else, which makes you feel socially included. You remain neatly packaged in the minds of others as someone who is agreeable. But the sad truth is that being described as agreeable is not a compliment because it usually means you're holding back. Flying right under the radar is what we've been taught to do, but so *meh*. If you continue, you will get to the end of your life and ask, "What was all *that* for?" or better yet, "*Who* was all that for?"

Perhaps the most painful part of risking criticism is that the ones who love you most are going to have the hardest time with any "stepping out" you choose to do, so whatever you do, don't try to convert your friends or family right away to your new way of living and thinking. It will be too much. Believe me—I tried it. And it was ugly. They will resist you. You will be seen as one of those bible-thumping, my-way-or-the-highway type crazy people. And that's the last thing you need right now. Don't let the fear of being the black sheep stop you! The white sheep secretly wish they had the guts to be you. For now, just take two Tylenol and keep on truckin'.

Day 5: Risk Criticism or Face Mediocrity

⊙ Questions to Ponder:

What do you really, really, really want?

_____
_____
_____
_____

Who in your life would stay with you no matter what?

_____
_____
_____
_____

◆ Thought to Think:

I am doing what's best for me. I am SO done with mediocre. (You can amuse yourself by saying this with a Valley Girl accent.)

⚙ Action to Take:

If you have a naysayer in your life, put them on the back burner until you're strong enough to tell them how you really feel. Actions speak louder than words. The more solid you become in your new skin, the more they'll believe you. If the critic is someone who's not a true friend, maybe they shouldn't be in your life anyway.

Fully Engaged

Watch this video in which a neuroscientist talks about the realness of social pain, to understand why stepping out hurts: https://www.youtube.com/watch?v=NNhk3owF7RQ.

DAY 6

You Are More Than Your Circumstances

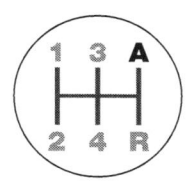

"All things splendid have been achieved by those who dared believe that something inside them was superior to circumstance."

Bruce Barton

A magnet with that quotation sticks on the side of my fridge, matching perfectly with the black and white (and red) décor of our kitchen; yet it does not blend in at all. I notice it every day and I'm reminded that circumstance, the life that surrounds me, is nothing more than what I've created it to be. We are creators of our own reality, our eyes (and brains) serving as the filters through which our thoughts and feelings make the world, seeing it as we are, not as it is.

Fully Engaged

Because there is no world without our filters, perception *is* reality. When we understand that no circumstance is a coincidence, and assume a creative role in our life, we take back our power and use it for positive change, to be, do and have what we always thought was "out there."

Speaking of "out there"—we've been tricked into thinking that something "out there" has caused us to be miserable and lonely "in here" with our thoughts, whether they're of our mothers, teachers, preachers, children, bosses, our financial situations, our jobs, our cars. All the things the therapist stirs up out of your subconscious mind. Some of us pop pills and pound cocktails to mask our depression and anxiety.

Our excuse for not being the joyful and fulfilled beings we're meant to be is too often "somebody else" or "something else." The finger is always pointed elsewhere, as if the responsibility and the burden of your life is not on you. Stop the madness and point at yourself. Yes, do it now. And say, "It's up to me to be who I want to be!"

Pointing at others or at circumstance is simply a way to take away the pain of not having what you want.

This is not a book about *blaming* yourself (or anybody or anything else) for where you are in life. It's about owning the fact that YOU are a powerful being and creator, full of untapped potential who deserves the very best that life has to offer. Misery is optional. Accountability is not.

Day 6: You Are More Than Your Circumstances

Questions to Ponder:

What circumstances in your life are driving you bat-shit crazy?

_____
_____
_____
_____

What circumstances in your life make you genuinely happy?

_____
_____
_____
_____

Thought to Think:

I am rising above my circumstances and creating the life I've always wanted.

Action to Take:

Unwanted circumstances typically don't come on all of a sudden, but are instead a result of small steps, small decisions you make over and over again. Ponder that and make a new decision today to start turning a circumstance in your life around. This is challenging because it's like training to run a marathon when you've barely run a 5K. It will take you a

Fully Engaged

while to get there, but each step will get you closer. Be patient and do something today that can make even a small dent in your dissatisfaction.

DAY 7

Freedom vs. Discipline

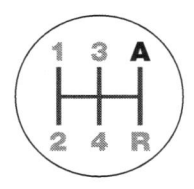

> *"Some people regard discipline as a chore. For me, it is a kind of order that sets me free to fly."*
> **Julie Andrews**

I've been a free spirit since my early childhood, and I've always sought every possible opportunity to experience something new and different. My mother may be partially to blame for encouraging me: since I was an "all-over-the-place" child, she would introduce me as her "free spirited child" as I ran and jumped and skipped and played around her company and their conversations. I felt excused for not being still for one second, for running before I ever walked.

Fully Engaged

This free-flying selfie is a part of me that I REALLY love and appreciate. But it can also be my Achilles' heel. This part of me has landed me in faraway places, been the impetus for learning a new language, and helped me push past many self-imposed limits. On the other hand, this free-spirited self has also led me to jump quickly from one thing to another, leaving little time for consistent action and discipline. Sometimes this makes me feel scattered, shallow, and bored if chaos is not the order of the day.

As Julie Andrews was aware, discipline has the power to engender freedom. As I grow, I learn that discipline is not always binding, but instead it's often freeing. Balancing that free-spirited self with some rules and regulations for engagement and some genuine boundaries has certainly made me freer in many regards.

For example, I've never been a fan of budgeting or dealing much with money at all. As long as I had everything I needed for the moment, I avoided the topic and spent without much thinking. Fortunately, I've always had enough (though sometimes barely) but wasn't in the habit of saving or thinking about my future. I would say I always had a flying-by-the-seat-of-my-pants approach to finances.

I had finally had enough of monthly payments (and having more month than my paycheck) so Chris and I created a monthly budget. Though it hasn't been easy or super-fun,

Day 7: Freedom vs. Discipline

it HAS been extremely rewarding: we now have a plan for our money that's already producing great results. We've cleared all of our debt (except for our mortgage and one student loan). We pay cash for everything—no more financing or "12-months-interest-free" for us. We save for things instead. We've been able to cash flow home renovations, medical expenses, and other things that in the past we would've had to finance. And discipline in our budgeting has opened up our communication as a couple and made us more disciplined in other areas of our lives as well. We have come a looooonnnnggg way…although we still have a ways to go.

This type of discipline also works well in other areas of life. Having a plan and sticking to it is one of the hardest things to do because of our demanding desire for instant gratification. But pushing through and maintaining control is way more rewarding than the temporary pleasure of eating that piece of chocolate cake or hitting the snooze button instead of going on a run.

Questions to Ponder:

Where can you be more disciplined in your life?

_____
_____
_____
_____

What is a new habit you'd like to create?

_____
_____
_____
_____

Thought to Think:

I am disciplined, which leads me to freedom.

Action to Take:

Do something at 110 percent today, taking NO shortcuts. Resolve to spend the next thirty-odd days being disciplined about using this book as a part of your daily routine. Map out a plan for yourself and stick to it.

Creating a new discipline or habit in one area of life often creates a ripple effect in other areas. Charles Duhigg in his

Day 7: Freedom vs. Discipline

book The Power of Habit calls these "keystone habits." In other words, being disciplined to read and reflect in your journal with this book will likely lead to you creating positive habits in other areas of your life.

Read more about keystone habits in this article and get Charles Duhigg's book if you want to learn more: http://experiencelife.com/article/the-power-of-habit/.

Learn more about getting out of debt and budgeting at: http://www.daveramsey.com/home/

DAY 8

Is Compassion Overrated?

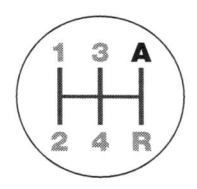

"If you want others to be happy, practice compassion. If you want to be happy, practice compassion."
Dalai Lama

Of course other people want you to be compassionate because it benefits them. You being nice can make them feel accepted and loved. But what about you? Are you compassionate towards yourself? Probably not. Most people say and do things to themselves that they would NEVER say or do to someone else. This has been a REAL eye-opener for me, a recovering self-hater. As someone who always wanted to please other people and make sure they were happy and taken care of, I left little time to love myself in the process. Unlike a mother comforting her crying child, I often ridicule myself when I'm feeling less than perfectly happy.

Practice being kind to yourself and giving yourself a break BEFORE doing that for others. If you give all your compassion away, you won't have enough left for yourself. You'll feel depleted and tired with no energy to be compassionate towards others anyway, and any false attempt to do so will be transparent. Being fake takes a helluva lot more energy than being YOU.

When it comes to compassion: First you, then them. I know. This is going to be a tough one because this goes against everything that is engrained in your DNA and in the manners you were taught growing up. If you need some inspiration, just look at a man in your life. It's likely that he takes care of himself first and then others. I'm not knocking men (or praising them, particularly)—just helping you find some evidence that this *is* possible.

I'm saying that compassion is *not* overrated—but sometimes it is misdirected. You have to focus some of that kindness and generosity inwards. If you aren't being compassionate to yourself FIRST, being compassionate to others won't feel quite as warm.

Day 8: Is Compassion Overrated?

⊙ Questions to Ponder:

What unkind things do you say and think to yourself that you would NEVER say to another person?

_____
_____
_____
_____

What do you think you can do to be more compassionate towards yourself today?

_____
_____
_____
_____

Thought to Think:

I am compassionate towards myself first and then with others.

Action to Take:

When you catch yourself saying something really nasty to yourself today, say "delete" and replace it with something kinder. Example: "My arms look so flabby. DELETE... My arms are perfectly imperfect. I am happy just the way I am."

Fully Engaged

Read this short article on the benefits of self-compassion: http://well.blogs.nytimes.com/2011/02/28/go-easy-on-yourself-a-new-wave-of-research-urges/

DAY 9
Your I AM Super Power

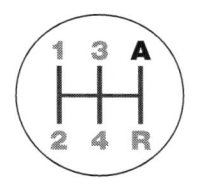

"Whatever follows I AM will come looking for you."
Joel Osteen

It is said that the two most powerful words in the English language are "I AM." When we say those two tiny words we conjure the creative, all-knowing spirit within ourselves that is connected to something much bigger than we can ever imagine. We talked about being self-compassionate yesterday, and I'm going to take that idea a little further now.

We are all part of this great big Universe created by an omniscient, omnipresent energy (God, Jesus, Buddha, Allah, or something else—the name doesn't matter). We are part of it,

Fully Engaged

so we must be made of the same spiritual stuff that all creation is made of—the *god juju,* we'll call it—and we are that creative pulse of and for infinity. In other words, within us is the power of the whole universe. Mind boggling, huh?

So, now that you know that, anything you put after I AM becomes a creative pulse in the universe, a spark to ignite a flame of possibility. Most people use these words to their detriment since most of us don't talk very nicely to ourselves (remember yesterday's passage?). Or most people use I AM with NOT—but NOT isn't part of the god juju's vocabulary. If you say *I am NOT creative,* what the universe hears is *I am creative.* Now that sounds like music to my ears. But if you say *I am NOT defensive,* the universe hears *I am defensive.* Uh-oh. You may want to turn that one around. Anytime you use the words I AM, you are making a bold statement to the universe. Do it once, no big deal—maybe. Do it over and over again, and as Buddha said, you will become it!

Questions to Ponder:

How are you using I AM?

_____
_____
_____
_____

Day 9: Your I AM Super Power

What are your thoughts/feelings about being part of god juju?

_____
_____
_____
_____

Thought to Think:

I am a powerful, creative force in the universe.

Action to Take:

Notice where you use the word NOT and remember that the god juju doesn't recognize it. Also, the god juju doesn't know subjects. If you say something about someone else (You are_____; She is_____), you're really talking about yourself since we're all connected via the god juju. Remember that the next time you criticize someone. If you stop being so hard on everyone else, you'll be lighter on yourself too. And vice versa.

Go here to view Oprah's LifeClass with Joel Osteen on the power of I AM: http://www.oprah.com/oprahs-lifeclass/Oprah-and-Joel-Osteen-I-Am-Life-Is-How-You-See-It

DAY 10
Affirming You're Awesome

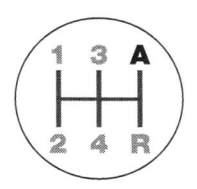

> *"I AM is a feeling of permanent awareness. The very center of consciousness is the feeling of I AM. I may forget who I am, where I am, what I am, but I cannot forget that I AM. The awareness of being remains, regardless of the degree of forgetfulness of who, where, and what I AM."*
>
> **Neville Goddard, *The Power of Awareness***

Coming to know the power of "I AM" has been one of the more impactful journeys of my life. Since I've begun to understand that I create my reality through my thoughts, feelings and actions, the idea of using "I AM" to manifest my destiny makes perfect sense to me. So if you want an awesome life, you have to not only say—but also KNOW—that you're awesome (and, yes, imperfect)!

To be happier, we have to be able to see ourselves in our mind's eye as happy and fulfilled. Maxwell Maltz, author of the 1960s bestselling book *PsychoCybernetics,* said, "Change the self image and you change the personality and the behavior." Maltz and other happiness experts tell us that what we *think* about ourselves directly affects our behaviors, attitudes and actions. Makes sense to me.

One of the best ways to improve the way we feel about ourselves and to boost our happiness levels is through affirmations, positive statements about ourselves. Affirmations make us feel better because they build our confidence and belief in ourselves. And they're necessary! We are powerful creators who sometimes forget our self-worth and therefore we can be downright mean to ourselves sometimes. We wake up in the morning and bash our bodies and wrinkles. We go to bed thinking that we haven't accomplished enough.

Affirmations help us remember who we are and who we want to become. Speak your affirmations ten times in the morning and ten times at night while looking at yourself in the mirror. And read Louise Hay's book *You Can Heal Your Life*—as far as I'm concerned, it's the bible on building self-worth through affirmations.

Day 10: Affirming You're Awesome

However, if all you do is look in the mirror and do affirmations, nothing will change. Build some confidence, but even before it's fully built, start to DO things that exude and require confidence—that will help you build it further. Intentionally stretch outside of your comfort zone. Volunteer to lead a project. Tell someone how you *really* feel. Run an extra mile. Ultimately, *acting* will get you further than just mentally encouraging yourself.

Questions to Ponder:

Where do you lack confidence in your life?

_____
_____
_____
_____

What can you DO today to stretch yourself outside your comfort zone and BOOST your confidence?

_____
_____
_____
_____

Thought to Think:

I am affirming my good all day, every day, and building my self-esteem.

Action to Take:

Write three positive affirmations here and repeat them to yourself ten times in the mirror. Repeat daily till you finish this book. Feel free to change them when you see fit. See what happens.

1. I am _____.

2. I am _____.

3. I am _____.

If you want to learn more about the power of affirmations, visit Louise Hay's website: http://www.louisehay.com

DAY 11
Putting a Fence Up Around Your Life

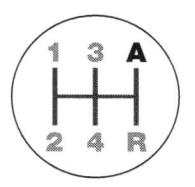

"Life begins at the end of your comfort zone."
Neale Donald Walsch

Driving around town the other day, I noticed some really good-looking fences around people's yards; some were traditional white-washed picket fences, and others were tall, black, and formal. They just seemed so darned perfect and created a nice protective boundary from the outside world. Fine for a house—but not for your life.

Seeing them made me question how often we put fences up around our lives, not allowing ourselves to move beyond the boundaries of our own habits, behaviors and thoughts, fearing the vulnerability that lies just outside of our comfort zone. Though some boundaries are healthy (for example, asking your in-laws to call before popping in, or saying "no" to an invitation to a swingers party—unless you're a swinger), staying in your comfort zone will stagnate you and keep you from the growth and unbridled joy you truly deserve.

Having boundaries and breaking them down is an example of a "healthy tension." Only you (the BIG you—not the excuse-ridden ego that lives in your head) know what the healthy tension is. You don't want to put the boundaries too high, but you don't want them too low either where you become a doormat.

Questions to Ponder:

What fence are you ready to take down?

_____
_____
_____
_____

Day 11: Putting a Fence Up Around Your Life

One a scale of 1 to 10, 10 being outstanding, how good are you with having appropriate boundaries? What would make you a 10?

_____
_____
_____
_____

Thought to Think:

I have healthy boundaries and move outside of my comfort zone.

Action to Take:

Move outside of your fenced-in life today. Go outside your comfort zone. Accept an invitation you would normally turn down, try a food you've never ordered, or buy some sparkly shoes. At the same time, explore some new boundaries you'd like to set. Say "no" instead of "yes" or be more vocal than you ever have before.

DAY 12

No More Either/Or. Instead, I'll Have Both

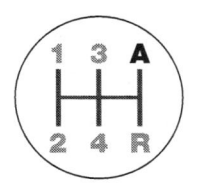

There are two kinds of people in the world: those who think there are two kinds of people in the world and those who don't.

I used to LOATHE tests where the multiple-choice answers were:

A. This answer
B. That answer
C. Both A and B
D. Neither A nor B

Fully Engaged

These days, though, my answer is "C." Our whole lives we've been brainwashed into believing that this is an either/or world. French fries or Tater Tots. Soup or salad. Black or white. Success or failure. Life or death. Very rarely are things so cut-and- dried. Stop looking at life as a "one-right-answer" question. You can choose more than one or none of if you want to. Not making a decision is also a decision. Heck, you can turn your multiple-choice question into an essay and write your own answer. Bottom line is, this habit of limiting ourselves eats away at our spirits and makes us think we are pigeonholed into one right or wrong answer in other areas of our life.

This "lack-type" thinking reminds me of our tendency to delay pleasure. Thanks to my friend Erin who posed this question: "Why do we save our good china for special occasions, or that one-of-a-kind bottle of wine for future events that may never happen?"

Chris and I received a bottle of Dom Perignon for our wedding in 2006. That bottle sat in the back of our fridge for years before I finally decided to take it over to a friend's house to have with dinner. Why didn't we do that sooner? My Dad and I visited Italy in 2003 and bought my grandmother some beautiful Murano glasses to drink her toddies from. They're still stored in her cabinet and God only knows when they'll see the light of day. In the meantime she still uses the same plain-Jane glasses from the 1950s.

Day 12: No More Either/Or. Instead, I'll Have Both

This type of "holding out" assumes that in the future we'll be more worthy to experience this or that. Why not show the universe that you know you're worthy, and open yourself to other similar windfalls?

This isn't an insult to those of us who "hold out." It's just an opportunity to ask ourselves: What are we waiting for? We don't really need to wait, do we?

Questions to Ponder:

Where are you being too "either/or" about in your life?

_____
_____
_____
_____

What have you been holding on to, to use for a special occasion?

_____
_____
_____
_____

🛢 Thought to Think:

I am done with "either/or living." I am decisive and clear about my future and what I want. Joy now is better than potential joy later!

⚙ Action to Take:

When you're out and about today, take the opportunity to have both, or to choose something different than you normally would. It takes deliberate practice to change and try new things. If you have something you've been saving for a special occasion, create an event (or a non-event) and use that thing you've been saving ASAP! Dust off your formal china and eat off it at dinner tonight.

DAY 13

Write Your Life

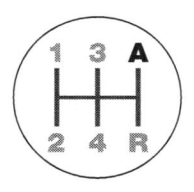

You are living your story.

You are the author of your life. Even though you might not have been writing your life on paper before this, you've been thinking, speaking, and acting in powerful ways that author—and alter—your life story. You're literally writing your story now since you've started this journey with me.

This is critical knowledge because it means that you understand you get to write your story the way that you want it, each and every moment. So now you're not just *thinking* about your story, but you're putting the pen to the paper, being sure to get it all down. As you are probably learning from this book, something magical happens when you take the thoughts from your head and feelings from your soul and give them physical form on paper. Yikes! (In a good way, right?)

Yes, feel free to write whatever you're thinking and feeling now. But stretch yourself—write about what you want your life to be outside of your current circumstances. For example, if you want a new job or to lose 20 pounds, write it down as though you already have it. An even more impactful way to do this is to use the words "I AM" in the present tense (like you did in the affirmation section!) with feeling and emotion behind each word.

Keep in mind: There's a healthy tension that has to take place between loving yourself and being content where you are, and dreaming and striving for more. If you use your future as a benchmark for your current happiness, you'll never be good enough. Give yourself a big bear hug and LOVE yourself genuinely no matter where you are, and then you can go for it!

I love to go back and read my old journals. I've been writing in my journal daily for the last seven years (and I wrote intermittently for years before that), and it's pretty unbelievable when I consider the things that have manifested, which once I only dreamed of. One of my favorite discoveries of the power of "writing my life" was from a journal I wrote in back in 2002. At the time I was living in Seville, Spain, and teaching Emi, a very special student who made a tremendous impact on me. In fact, I'm certain she taught me more about life than I ever taught her about English.

> *After so much time wondering what was wrong with me, I finally have figured out all that needed mending, nurturing was my spirit. I remember the day I realized this. I was having English class with Emi, a gastroenterologist, who I now consider to be the person, the soul who started my journey.*
>
> *I was telling her that I always had stomach aches and she told me that all digestive disorders were connected to one's mental state. I thought this sounded a little strange, but then realized that it really did make sense and that all of my recent stomach aches were actually my spirit letting me know it needed to be expressed, revealed, and developed. Since that conversation, my stomach problems have been minimal... nonexistent, actually.*
>
> *But that's not the most important part. Aside from relieving my stomach pains, the revealing of my spirit has caused me to look at the world differently, so I guess you could say that Emi has taught me to look at the world differently. She taught me how powerful love can be and how a person's life can change if he/she does everything for love. She has taught me about our souls, where we go after death, where we come from, and why we are the way we are.*

Fully Engaged

> *Emi has given me the starting point to take off on my journey. I will use all she has shared with me to build who I am, and just as she has done, I will use my knowledge and experience to change the lives of others. I hope that throughout this journey I remember how important it is to write. Maybe someday I will have enough experience to write my own book.*

Here I am. Years later. Writing book number two—of many!

Questions to Ponder:

What do you want your life to look like by this time next year? In five years? In ten years?

_____
_____
_____
_____

What do you love about life right now?

_____
_____
_____
_____

Day 13: Write Your Life

Thought to Think:

I am writing my life just the way I want it.

Action to Take:

Write about something that you really, really want to happen, a dream, a vision. Read it again before you go to sleep tonight. Mentally rehearse it in your mind. Re-write anything you want to change. And then read it again in the morning. Continue editing your story until it's just right.

Then go to http://www.futureme.org/ and write an email to your future self about what you really, really want to happen in six months or a year (or however long you choose!). The program will deliver your email (which you'll probably forget that you've written) and you can see how far you've come. Very cool!

DAY 14
60,000 – 50,000 – 80 – 95

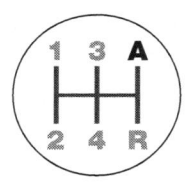

"Our life always expresses the result of our dominant thoughts."

Søren Kierkegaard

You have 60,000 thoughts per day. Of those 60,000 thoughts, the "average" person has 50,000 negative thoughts. Or, 80 percent crapshoot thoughts. Worse than that, 95 percent of the thoughts you have today will be the same you had yesterday—and you'll have them again tomorrow. Repeated shit. No wonder so many people are sick, depressed, suicidal and angry. This epidemic of negative thinking has got to stop for us to be the tremendous people we are here to be. This is yet another example why being "average" SUCKS!

Fully Engaged

I'm sure you've heard this before, but I'll say it again. If you want to be different, you have to *think* differently. Being mostly positive to create the results you want in your life isn't hard, it's simply a new habit. Habits take time to form (have you looked up *The Power of Habit* by Charles Duhigg?).

Shifting those 80 percent negative thoughts into 51 percent positive thoughts creates a tipping point of huge change. Only 51 percent positive thoughts will create a chain reaction of events to shift your energy and the energy of those around you. Let me say it again. It's NOT HARD, JUST A CHOICE. It's a deliberate effort to recognize when you're being and feeling negative, and consciously choosing something more favorable. Or at the very least, noticing the thought. Most of us are unable to shift because we are unaware of our thinking.

Because of all the negativity we're exposed to, disciplined thinking takes deliberate and consistent action. Think of it as a *practice* and not as a destination. Some days you'll be better at it than others (because of course, nobody's perfect). Keep practicing. You will mess up, but don't give up!

Day 14: 60,000 – 50,000 – 80 – 95

Questions to Ponder:

What percentage of negative vs. positive thoughts do you think you have?

_____
_____
_____
_____

What can you do today to increase your positive thoughts by 10 percent?

_____
_____
_____
_____

Thought to Think:

I am becoming more and more positive every day, and my life is getting better and better.

Action to Take:

Write a description of your house, using the stream-of-consciousness technique. Spend ten minutes writing whatever words and phrases come to mind with no editing. Read the description. Congratulations! You now have a description of

Fully Engaged

your inner world. Our inner world creates our outer world. If your description pleases you, congratulations! If you're unhappy with it, get to cleaning!

DAY 15
Being "Normal" Sucks!

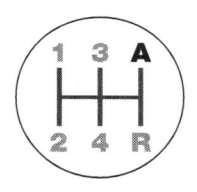

"'Status quo' is Latin for 'the mess we're in.'"
Ronald Reagan

The main reason I want you to think about the story and life you're writing in a more intentional, methodical way is because if you don't, you will fall into the status quo. And I do mean FALL in! In case you haven't noticed, "normal" these days is sick, broke, tired, and unhappy. According to the Brené Brown TED Talk on vulnerability, "We are the most in-debt, obese, addicted and *medicated* adult cohort in US history." All you have to do to find evidence is look around and listen to your complaining co-workers and friends, or watch the news. We have to turn this around... and that starts with you!

Fully Engaged

Gary Hamel and C.K. Prahalad, two business professors, wrote about an experiment in which four monkeys were put in a room with a tall pole with a bunch of bananas suspended from the top. One of the monkeys began the climb for the treats and when he reached for the banana, he got doused with cold water. The next monkey and the next tried, and the same thing happened. Eventually they gave up. Then a new group of monkeys entered the room. When one of the new monkeys attempted to go after the bananas, one of the original four pulled him back down. After a few more attempts and being dragged down each time, the new monkeys finally gave up too, even though they had never been doused by the water.

Don't be a monkey! If you don't try something new and different, and intentionally write your life the way you want it, you will become a monkey.

Sometimes I feel like we've all been tricked into compliance (aka misery) through overexposure to the media and advertising, and into thinking that we have to keep up with the lifestyles of the rich and famous we see on reality TV and in *People* magazine, just to fit in. I'll call bullshit on that one. Behind the façade of most people's keeping-up-with-the-Joneses life is a person who is unfulfilled and begging for a Cinderella story, someone or something to rescue her from the madness, so that she feels satisfied with life. You have the power to *rescue yourself*. (And you're doing that as you continue to work through this book!)

Day 15: Being "Normal" Sucks!

Questions to Ponder:

How have you let the status quo drag you down and keep you there?

_____
_____
_____
_____

What have you done in the past to break away from the pack?

_____
_____
_____
_____

Thought to Think:

I am escaping normal.

Action to Take:

Look around you at the people you love, strangers on the street, and everyone in between. Observe whether you see them living a meaningful existence or keeping even with the status quo. Take note of the people who seem to be "faking it." Do everything you can to be real today. Speak your truth. Question someone else's opinion.

DAY 16

There's No Such Thing as Small Change

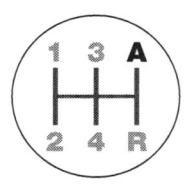

"Pain and pleasure govern us in all we do, in all we say, in all we think."

Jeremy Bentham

Your ability to adapt and change is perhaps your greatest asset. Evolution is good for the soul. Stagnation sucks! Flex your change muscles and get ready.

A man named John Fisher came up with a diagram to map out how we experience personal change. Google it or take a look at it here: http://www.businessballs.com/freepdfmaterials/fisher-transition-curve-2012bb.pdf

Really, the main thing you need to know is that when you go through change, you're going to feel like shit sometimes and you're going to feel great sometimes. Remember what it was like to learn to ride your bike or roller skate? Yep. Lots of skinned knees and elbows. Get your knee pads and helmets (and Tylenol) ready. Experiencing change is a roller-coaster ride and the highs (and lows) are only temporary.

And since we frequently dread the roller-coaster effect, we avoid change and new experiences. I'm sure you've heard of "pleasure seeking" and "pain avoidance." I don't want you to cut off your finger to feel the burn, but if you know up front that you're going to experience a range of emotions as you move through change, that awareness helps to pull you through. Too many people stay stuck in life because they are avoiding the pain, when if they'd work through that uncomfortable period, they'd reach a new level of pleasure and integration, as the Fisher curve shows us.

Questions to Ponder:

What emotions do you experience during change?

_____
_____
_____
_____

Day 16: There's No Such Thing as Small Change

What would you do if you knew you couldn't fail?

_____

_____

_____

_____

Thought to Think:

I am ready to make a positive change.

Action to Take:

What would you do if you knew you couldn't fail? Think about a small step you could take today to move towards that goal. It doesn't have to be anything big. If your imagination stalls on you here, just do a Google search or find a book to read on the topic or call someone who is an expert at what you want to do. If you can do something even a little more scary to get you there, do it. Your mantra today: Feel the fear and do it anyway.

Read about another interesting model for change and why you should try, try, try again even if at first you don't succeed: http://www.psychologytoday.com/blog/high-octane-women/201210/change-is-hard-heres-why-you-should-keep-trying

DAY 17
Henry Ford Jacked Us All Up

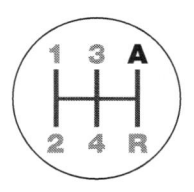

"Holding back is so close to stealing."

Neil Young

Henry Ford made a HUGE impact on the world. Without him, we would not be where we are today—and that is a both a blessing and a curse. I recently watched a documentary on Ford on PBS and was amazed by his focus and dedication to excellence. I was, however, also disappointed that he was such a jerk, with frigid family relationships and little care for the workers in his factory.

Using the Ford mass production model, we have maximized ourselves to the hilt, and automation can't get much cheaper or faster. We've figured out how to make 10,000

Fully Engaged

plastic baby dolls and 5,000 fake chicken fingers an hour. As rampant consumers we are grateful and now rely on other countries to fuel our needs (what the hell would we do without China or Bangladesh?).

Since we've offshored most manufacturing, we should be off to bigger and better and more meaningful things. But we're not. We're so scared to do something that will mess up the assembly line of normal that we hold ourselves back. Because of this mass-produced mentality, we have lost our art and pursuit of meaning. We are still not fully engaged in life.

Instead of being like everyone else in this factory of life, I want you to be distinctly yourself, to make your own unique contribution to the world. Something inside of you is like nothing that anyone else can offer. Buried under all the world's attempts at keeping you small and boring is your awesome sauce. Pile it on. We are ready to indulge!

Day 17: Henry Ford Jacked Us All Up

Questions to Ponder:

What did you love to be and do as a child?

_____
_____
_____
_____

Where do you think you're holding back from being you?

_____
_____
_____
_____

Thought to Think:

I am shining bright like a diamond.

Action to Take:

Do something today that you did often as a child. Ride your bike or climb a jungle gym. Read your favorite childhood book. Do anything it takes to remember what you loved then. I used to love cheerleading and speech contests. And that's pretty much what I do today (albeit in a somewhat more adult fashion and sans the toe touches and pyramids!).

DAY 18
Picking Yourself

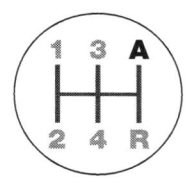

> *"Our cultural instinct is to wait to get picked. To seek out the permission, authority and safety that come from a publisher or a talk show host or even a blogger that says, 'I pick you.'"*
>
> **Seth Godin, *The Icarus Deception***

You're good enough, smart enough, and by golly, people like you! Whatever you can do today to "pick yourself" is going to get you light years ahead of waiting around for someone else to discover you on *American Idol*, Twitter or YouTube. Stop waiting around for your ship to come in. This is the loud and clear message of *The Icarus Deception*, one of my all-time-favorite Seth Godin books.

Fully Engaged

Seth himself demonstrated that he wasn't going to wait to get picked, by doing a Kickstarter campaign to convince his publisher to support a book that he was passionate about writing, but uncertain would appeal to his publisher. (Read more at http://www.kickstarter.com/projects/297519465/the-icarus-deception-why-make-art-new-from-seth-go

If you have an art to express (which you do—because everyone does) and you want to make something of it, you have to make the decision to go for it. You can't sit around and hope that somebody else will do the work for you.

When I decided to write this book, I didn't start by looking around to find a publisher or write a book proposal. I just started writing for 15-30 minutes every day (well, *kinda* every day), word by word, page by page. I had no idea what I'd do to promote my book and I didn't really care. I just did what I knew I could do, and I enjoyed it and allowed the rest to unfold! Yes, it did take hard work, diligence and dedication. But because I love writing and am living my purpose and my passion by writing this book—IT WAS WORTH IT! I'm sure your art is worth it, too. We get so focused on the end result sometimes that we forget there is so much JOY in the journey!

Day 18: Picking Yourself

Questions to Ponder:

What is your art?

_____
_____
_____
_____

How will you express it today?

_____
_____
_____
_____

Thought to Think:

I am expressing my art and picking myself!

Action to Take:

Read Seth Godin's book The Icarus Deception. That might take (more than) a minute, so in the meantime, watch the trailer to his book (http://www.youtube.com/watch?v=ZxQy8RJi1u8) and then spend ten minutes working on your art. If you can, share it with someone else. If it's not ready after ten minutes, spend at least ten more minutes on it tomorrow and the next day, until it's done.

DAY 19
Steamy Desire

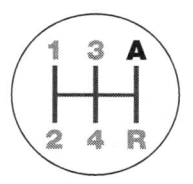

"The size of your success is measured by the strength of your desire; the size of your dream; and how you handle disappointment along the way."
Robert Kiyosaki

Wanting will never go away no matter how hard you try. Desire is the creative pulse of the universe and the impetus for real change. The tension of desire between where you are and where you want to be drives you to new levels of awesomeness.

When you want something different and feel that initial twinge of "but damn, I'm not there" or "I don't have it," be excited because this is the beginning of growth and development. This momentary discomfort is the starting point for change. You have to feel that tension to live with intention. Your frustrations and doubts are part of the process of getting from here to there. I bet you're feeling them right now. Embrace it!

By all means, have goals, go for things that you want. But I beg you, do not get so uncomfortable not having what you want that you give up entirely or make stupid decisions to speed up the process (i.e., maxing out your American Express). Quick fixes typically don't turn out well, as I've learned the hard way (i.e., a maxed out American Express). Desire is the creative pulse of the universe. Treat it that way.

Questions to Ponder:

What have you always wanted to be, do or have?

_____
_____
_____
_____

Day 19: Steamy Desire

How can you practice patience and discernment on the road to getting there?

_____
_____
_____
_____

Thought to Think:

I am excited by my desires and allow them time and space to manifest.

Action to Take:

Sometimes the best things do come to those who wait—and definitely to those who allow. Practice delaying pleasure and making smart decisions about getting what you want. When you see something that you really, really want, walk away from it—or do like I do and put it in your cart and drive it around the store for a minute and then take it out before you get in the checkout line. For some reason, walking around with it in the cart (or leaving it in your virtual cart if you shop online) is a good way to "try it on" and decide whether or not it is a need or a want.

DAY 20

Living in a Material World Is SOOOOO Eighties

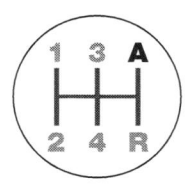

"We buy things we don't need with money we don't have to impress people we don't like."

Dave Ramsey

I'm a sucker for propaganda. Show me an advertisement with a gorgeous person sprawled out on a beach with a six-pack of abs (or beer!) and no matter what the ad is for, I want IT because I want to BE like that person. You're a sucka too; don't lie.

Modern day marketing relies heavily on fear and status as tools that make us all suckas. Until you stop and realize what's happening, you'll continue to be a sucka. Everyone

Fully Engaged

is trying to take your money by making you think you'll be happier, healthier, cooler, thinner, if you buy their product or service. In fact, many companies use those exact words in their brands, slogans, and ads to reel you in.

The important things in life are NOT things. And once you realize that there will always be something bigger and better no matter where you are, you can find peace in right now. Have you heard of the hedonic treadmill? This theory states that you will eventually return to your relative state of happiness after the temporary peaks and valleys of a negative or positive life event wear off.

Stop saying "If only this or that then I will be _____" (insert pleasant adjective). Believe me, I know this is hard. I am the one who maxed out an AmEx to ensure there were no voids in my life. (Side note—it didn't work). Getting that next great thing won't complete you. You may get a momentary rush when you buy that new purse or piece of art (I still do, for goodness sakes), but in the long run it will blend in just like everything else and just be another *thing*. Don't be a sucka.

Day 20: Living in a Material World Is SOOOOO Eighties

Questions to Ponder:

When was the last time you were a sucker for an advertisement?

_____
_____
_____
_____

What material thing do you really, really want that you can put off for a couple months?

_____
_____
_____
_____

Thought to Think:

I am leaving plenty of space for wonderful new opportunities to present themselves.

Action to Take:

Leave some space in your life for something unexpected and wonderful to come in. Don't look to fill up every moment and every free space available with all the crap you see on TV infomercials or in magazines. And if you have a storage space with loads of stuff in it—you really need to check yourself.

Fully Engaged

Make some room, leave your life to be, and see what happens. Look at ads and laugh because you're smarter than falling for any old scheme! And if you really need some inspiration, watch one of those hoarder shows on TV. Ick!

Learn more about the managing your money and getting out of debt at http://www.daveramsey.com/home/

DAY 21

Ditch the Pursuit of Perfection

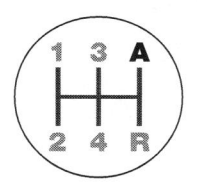

> *"Perfectionism is a defensive move. It's the belief that if we do things perfectly and look perfect, we can minimize or avoid the pain of blame, judgment, and shame."*
>
> **Brené Brown, *Daring Greatly***

Hi, my name is Adair, and I'm a recovering perfectionist. Phew. That felt good. Now you try it:

Hi, my name is _____, and I am a recovering perfectionist.

Ahhh.

Fully Engaged

I care WAY too much about how I look, how my house looks, and even how my husband's hair looks. When anyone is coming over, whether it's my best friend or the folks who clean my house, I rush around to organize my mail and hide away the clutter as if I have a point to prove—that my life is perfect and my house is fresh from the pages of Pottery Barn all the time. B.S.!

In my endless pursuit of perfection, I am never satisfied. (Isn't there a song about that by the Rolling Stones?) In this state of not being satisfied, I fall for every gimmick and say, "I want that" (and usually go out and get it), thinking that this "thing" will get me one step closer to perfection (remember yesterday's passage?). Aside from the financial repercussions (the toll on my pocketbook), the mental and emotional consequences of never feeling quite "perfect enough" are much more damaging.

It's important to desire more and better. That is what keeps the juices of life flowing (and our free-market society thriving). But it's critical to balance that desire with gratitude and appreciation (here's one of those balancing act moments I referenced earlier), noticing the little things that bring joy and finding contentment in the ordinary. Being grateful for the way life is right now. Seeing the perfection in imperfection. Saying, "Wow, aren't I lucky to have and be all of THIS?" every once in a while.

Day 21: Ditch the Pursuit of Perfection

Get off that treadmill (unless you're actually exercising). Stop peering at the Joneses. All is well and life is good. The pursuit of perfection is bogus. Everybody has their highs and lows. Nobody is perfect. And your life is pretty damn awesome just the way it is now. And it will continue to be more and more wonderful as you engage more fully in it!

Questions to Ponder:

On a scale of 1 to 10, 10 being "crazed by perfectionism," where do you rate yourself?

_____
_____
_____
_____

What do you need to do to think differently about perfectionism?

_____
_____
_____
_____

Thought to Think:

I am grateful for who and where I am right now.

Action to Take:

Make a gratitude list of five things you are grateful for. Do this every day for the next week (and the next and the next). In fact, do this every day for the rest of your life, and you will feel happier and more fulfilled. This very simple process has now evolved into my daily 20-30 minute solitude/journal time, which has slowly but surely transformed my life in ways I never believed possible. (And it also led to the writing of this book, and my previous one, Live with Intention.)

DAY 22

Being Grateful "As Is"

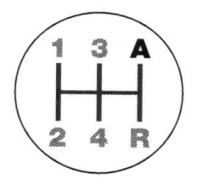

> *"The world is full of people looking for spectacular happiness while they snub contentment."*
>
> **Doug Larson**

While steamy desire—and the tension it creates—is a good thing, accepting and embracing where we are now is just as fantastic. Contentment is beautiful. It brings so much inner peace to our otherwise chaotic world. If you want to feel good, you must practice radical acceptance of now. Now, this fleeting moment in between here and there, is all we have.

If, in our pursuit for more and different and better, we forget to look around us and bless the goodness that's already here, we will never feel truly fulfilled. Remember when your "here" was your "there"? I sure as hell do. I thought that being "here" would solve all sorts of the issues I had while I was "there." It didn't turn out to be so. Because this *here* and this *now* bring on new burdens. Yes, many aspects of my life are much improved, but I still have my struggles. That's why gratitude and grace are powerful tools for creating a life we love.

Research proves that gratitude not only fuels, but also sustains, happiness. Martin Seligman, the founder of Positive Psychology, found that students who wrote a gratitude letter, and then visited the subject to read the letter, sustained happiness long after the appointment. Studies show that for a full month after a person reads the gratitude letter to the recipient, happiness levels go up, while boredom and other negative feelings decrease. The gratitude visit is more effective than any other exercise in positive psychology.

Start your day by saying grace: Thank you, GOD! End your day by recounting all the things in your day that went well. Write in your gratitude journal. Send a hand-written thank you card to someone you love, filled with reasons you love them.

Day 22: Being Grateful "As Is"

Questions to Ponder:

Have you thanked someone today?

_____
_____
_____
_____

How do you express gratitude?

_____
_____
_____
_____

Thought to Think:

I am grateful for the abundance of good in my life.

Action to Take:

Write a gratitude letter and schedule a time to read it to the person you wrote it to. Reap the benefits for a month! Read more about gratitude and positive psychology here: http://www.psychologytoday.com/articles/200602/make-gratitude-adjustment.

DAY 23
The World Behind the World

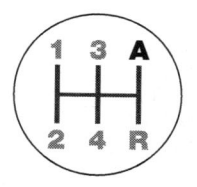

"There are no accidents... there is only some purpose that we haven't yet understood."

Deepak Chopra

So much amazing stuff happens in the world behind the physical world, yet we pay very little attention to it. We are so wrapped up in our stuff and our five senses that we forget the good spiritual and intuitive mojo all around us. Most of the world is invisible to us. Yet most of us are only thinking about what we have physical evidence for—things we are seeing, smelling, touching, tasting, hearing (or buying).

Some time ago in my journal, I decided to ask God to show me some serendipity. I had just heard a great story about

Fully Engaged

providence from a friend and wanted to see some for myself. I felt like it had been a long time since the stars had aligned just for me (though now I know that's my fault). So I asked, and it was given.

I was working a craft festival selling the small-batch soy candles I make (yosoycandles.com) when I noticed a lovely lady walking towards our booth wearing the *exact* shirt that I had pondered wearing that day. This would be no big deal if the shirt were readily available, like something from Gap or J. Crew, but it was a shirt that I had bought in Barcelona, made of fabric from a Cirque du Soleil costume. Uncommon, to say the least. When this woman came to smell the candles, I ended up telling her my serendipity story and she was so kind. It was her birthday, so I gifted her one of our candles as my homage to the universe. She was a special soul that I was destined to meet! Since then, I've come to find out she was also an author and truth-seeker. Thank you, God!

I thought I was done with serendipity for the day. But later as I browsed the crafts fair, I saw a print that I've been dreaming up in my head for a long time. Without explanation, the phrase *joie de vivre* often came to mind. I've always thought that a realization of this concept would make a nice picture for our wall. I had been thinking about it just that morning and *BAM*—there it was. The even-better ending to the story was that I bartered two candles for it—no cash exchange at all! Now it hangs on our wall as a nice reminder that serendipity is always here.

Day 23: The World Behind the World

Questions to Ponder:

What are your feelings about serendipity?

_____
_____
_____
_____

When is the last time you had a serendipitous experience? What was it?

_____
_____
_____
_____

Thought to Think:

I am opening space to allow more serendipity.

Action to Take:

Set an intention to attract something serendipitous today. Don't be attached to what it is, just ask to receive something that when it comes your way you'll know it's not some lowly coincidence, but the result of something larger sending you a special message.

DAY 24

Brain Connections

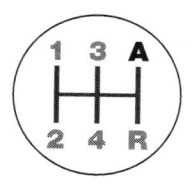

> *"If we think the world is a dangerous place, we look around for evidence of this and find it. If we think people are talking about us, we find evidence for this too. Whatever filter we hold in mind, the brain looks for evidence to confirm this filter, and it does this extremely efficiently, second to second, without our conscious mind being aware of what we are doing."*
> **David Rock**

Inside your head all kinds of fascinating things are taking place above and below the surface. Connections are firing in your brain as you read this and as you experience the world. These connections help you make sense of the world and stay safe and comfortable (most of the time). As efficiently as possible, your brain receives information and does everything it can to hardwire the connections that occur so it can spend the rest of its time being lazy.

The most fascinating part of learning even just a little bit about the brain is that it takes all the "airy-fairy" stuff that I've been living (and preaching) about how our thoughts create our reality, and cements it in science. Boy, am I ever excited about that. Basically your brain acts as a giant filter and it's up to you as to what type of filter you want it to be. This is why, if you want something new and different, you have to *think* differently to open your filter. By doing this, you start to notice new people, new things, and new opportunities that are aligned with the new direction you're headed.

Have you ever had the experience of getting something new (perhaps a car or new shoes) and then suddenly notice that everyone has the same thing? That's because you've opened your filter. I was absolutely convinced of this filtering when we started trying to get pregnant. Suddenly I saw baby bumps and newborns everywhere. Yes, those circumstances were always around me, but I hadn't noticed them. My filter was different so my experience was different.

Day 24: Brain Connections

Questions to Ponder:

What old rut are you ready to rewire?

_____
_____
_____
_____

Think of a time you had an "aha!" moment. What did you do differently from that point on?

_____
_____
_____
_____

Thought to Think:

I am building new connections to be, do, and have what I want.

Action to Take:

Open up your brain filter by focusing on something for the day; a certain kind of car or shoe (or whatever you want) and see if you begin to notice more of what you're focusing on. If you don't, give yourself a few days and see what happens. Read more about changing your brain to change you life at http://www.drjoedispenza.com/index.php?page_id=home and http://www.neuroleadership.org/index.shtml

DAY 25

Action to Create New Habits

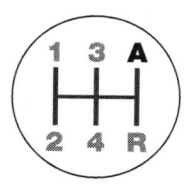

> *"Science is showing it's not that difficult to bridge the gap between a thought and a habit. If we want to hardwire a new behavior we just need to give our mental map enough attention, over enough time, to ensure it becomes embedded in our brain."*
>
> **David Rock**

When my husband and I moved to Atlanta a few years ago, we had a tennis court a block from our house. After many days of walking past the courts and saying, "Someday we're going to play tennis," we finally bought racquets and made it happen. The first times we played, we were TERRIBLE and quickly exhausted by all the ball-chasing. We still somehow managed to hit and return one or two good shots here and there, which motivated us to continue playing. We are fairly athletic and love a good competition (especially my husband), so this was a new version of fun for us.

Little by little we were able to rally more. Then I moved from hitting only forehand shots to trying some backhand shots. First with one hand, then with two. Again, an awkward transition, but a couple of good shots energized me enough to keep me trying again and again. I will always remember the day that we "spontaneously" decided to start serving and actually playing games. I didn't even know how to keep score! The day before I had watched a chick serving; she wasn't doing anything fancy, but could get it over the net and in the box. I thought to myself, "I can do that!" My serve evolved much like my game did (and it's now pretty darn good and imperfect).

Eventually we got good enough to play challenging games together. We got better equipment, new shoes, and our skills continued to improve. We attended tennis clinics and doubles round robins.

We taught ourselves to play tennis one baby-step at a time. Those initial phases were sometimes uncomfortable and not a whole lot of fun (remember the change curve?), but now our games are extremely enjoyable and tennis has become part of our lives as a couple.

Day 25: Action to Create New Habits

I would say one thing Chris and I do well is start things. And the things that we enjoy, we continue to pursue. The things we don't enjoy, we drop. I used to look at this as a bad thing because my parents made me take piano lessons, gymnastics, and ballet, and NOT quit even after it wasn't fun (at least not during the season). If you don't start something and go through the discomfort of not being good, you'll never be on a new adventure. And no adventure = boring!

Questions to Ponder:

What new activity have you tried that you sucked at in the beginning?

_____
_____
_____
_____

What feelings do you associate with learning something new?

_____
_____
_____
_____

Fully Engaged

Though to Think:

I am patient with myself when trying new things.

Action to Take:

Try a new activity that you are completely unfamiliar with for the next month.

Notice how you feel from the beginning until the end and what thoughts cross your mind as you learn the new activity. Reflect on where you started and where you ended. Learn more about the four stages of learning here: http://www.managetrainlearn.com/page/conscious-competence-ladder

DAY 26

Why Practice for Seven Hours When You Can Visualize for One?

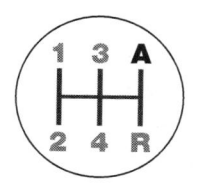

"Ordinary people believe only in the possible. Extraordinary people visualize not what is possible or probable, but rather what is impossible. And by visualizing the impossible, they begin to see it as possible."

Cherie Carter-Scott

Australian psychologist Alan Richardson conducted a little experiment on visualization. He chose a group of random students (not basketball players), divided them into three groups, and benchmarked each student's ability to make free throws. Then:

- The first group practiced free throws for 20 minutes every day.
- The second group didn't practice or visualize making free throws.
- The third group only spent twenty minutes a day visualizing themselves making free throws, but no practice was allowed.

What do you think happened as a result? (You probably have a good idea from the title.) There was a 23 percent improvement in the accuracy of the students who *only* visualized and a 24 percent improvement in the accuracy of the students who actually practiced making free throws. No improvement in the group that neither visualized nor practiced.

We underestimate our power. Seeing something in our mind's eye absolutely takes us closer to making it happen. Mental rehearsal is a powerful tool in living a meaningful life. Because you have many habits that you're likely not excited about continuing, visualization can help you reroute those habits into something more aligned with your ideal self.

For example, if you feel stuck in the realm of relationships, start envisioning yourself as having a positive and fun relationship. Seeing it in your head will help you feel more comfortable with the new possibilities you seek. And

Day 26: Why Practice for Seven Hours When You Can Visualize for One?

seeing it in your head allows your brain (which is nothing more than a giant filter) to see more.

I had a powerful experience with visualization right before my first book came out. One of authors and speakers I admire most is Jack Canfield (co-author of the *Chicken Soup for the Soul* series), and I wanted to meet him and show him my book. So I decided to test out visualization (since I had just read about its power) and began to spend ten minutes every day for several weeks envisioning the conversation I'd have with him and showing him my book. I knew I'd have the opportunity to see him at an empowerment seminar I'd be attending, so the timing was perfect. All I did was close my eyes and imagine our conversation. No big deal. No attachment. On the morning of the seminar my mom and I were sitting in the lobby of the hotel and Jack Canfield walked through, all alone, with no one else around. I jumped out of my seat with my manuscript and proceeded to have the exact same conversation with him that I'd been playing out in my head. I showed him my book and he eventually wrote a testimonial for my first book, *Live with Intention*. This was a big moment for me in many ways, but most powerful because I learned that visualization WORKS!

Questions to Ponder:

What are you seeing in your life that you're not excited about?

_____
_____
_____
_____

What would you like to see instead?

_____
_____
_____
_____

Thought to Think:

I am seeing myself as I want to be.

Action to Take:

Set a timer for 15 minutes and imagine yourself being, doing or having something (or someone) you really, really want. Immerse yourself in the scene using all five senses to heighten the experience. Take note of how you feel when you're done. To learn more about creative visualization, go here: http://www.shaktigawain.com/products/books/creative-visualization

DAY 27

Subconsciously Rewiring Your Thoughts

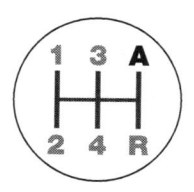

"Your subconscious is a powerful and mysterious force which can either hold you back or help you move forward. Without its cooperation, your best goals will go unrealized; with its help, you are unbeatable."

Jenny Davidow

While we're on the fascinating topic of creative visualization, I have to talk about the subconscious mind, because under-the-surface thoughts often block our greatest intentions to live a fully engaged life.

It is said that 90 percent of our thinking is subconscious. Because most of our life is on autopilot and most of our

Fully Engaged

thoughts and habits are not conscious, we are unaware that those unconscious thoughts could be running our lives and ruining our best efforts to be our best selves. Research shows that the intellect is only conscious of between twenty and fifty bits of information per second out of the millions taking place below its awareness (see *The User Illusion: Cutting Consciousness Down to Size* by Tor Nørretranders).

I've handled these prickly buggers in a number of ways, but my preferred method of eliminating subconscious blocks is hypnotherapy. No, not the kind where you get put under a spell so you bark like a dog or cluck like a chicken. I'm talking about the kind where a trained and benevolent practitioner puts you in an awake but dreamlike state where you can erase any negative blocks in your subconscious and replace them with positive thoughts and intentions.

A few years back when I was seeking a new job and wanted to perceive myself in a way that I'd be prepared to accept a higher-level position and salary, I used my hypnotherapist friend Jill to eliminate small thoughts I was having about myself and my career. Within three weeks of the session, I had a job offer on the table where I'd be making substantially more money, and more importantly, doing something that didn't feel like work at all.

I typically do this once or twice a year as I become conscious of goals I want to achieve and feel subconscious blocks

Day 27: Subconsciously Rewiring Your Thoughts

holding me back. Your subconscious mind is the piece of your mind that has a direct connection to God, the universe, or whatever you call the omniscient, omnipresent benevolence in the world. The more blocked we are, the less we feel this connection.

Questions to Ponder:

Would you be willing to try hypnotherapy? Why or why not?

_____
_____
_____
_____

Can you identify an area of your life where you feel a subconscious thought is blocking you?

_____
_____
_____
_____

Thought to Think:

I am done with any thoughts that are blocking my greatest attempts at meaning.

Fully Engaged

⚙️ Action to Take:

Go to http://powerfulhypnotherapy.com/ to learn more about how hypnotherapy can help you. All of my sessions with Jill have been over the phone and HIGHLY effective. If you're not quite ready for that, read more about ho'oponopono, an ancient Hawaiian form of hitting Ctrl+Alt+Del on your problems to allow something much bigger than you (God) to solve them for you.

This is a great introductory article. http://www.self-i-dentity-through-hooponopono.com/pdfs/who-english-abridged.pdf

DAY 28

Give People Their S@%* Back (figuratively and literally)

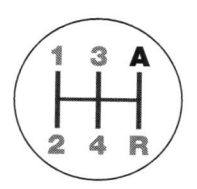

> "The meeting of two personalities is like the contact of two chemical substances: if there is any reaction, both are transformed."
>
> **C.G. Jung**

I recently did this activity in a hypnotherapy session with Jill and found it quite cathartic. You should do it too!

Imagine all the thoughts and feelings (aka *baggage*) that you've taken on for the purpose of empathizing with others... from your parents, siblings, needy friends, bosses, and strangers, about their break-ups, make-ups, job changes, and marriage problems. Dig deep (or as far as you need to go) and imagine cleaning out all the shit that you've taken on, both consciously and subconsciously, over the years. Now build it up from the ground into a pile in front of you. Watch it grow as you pile all the shit that's not yours, as high as it needs to grow. Maybe it's not very tall... or maybe it's as tall as a skyscraper (mine was!).

Seeing the pile on the ground clearly in front of you, encircle yourself with as many people as you feel appropriate—5, 10, 50, 1,000—all the people who have offered you their crud that you have chosen to take. One by one, take a handful of the sludge and give it back to each person saying, "Thank you. I love you," until the pile is gone.

See this in your mind's eye and a lifetime of burden will be lifted. Take a moment to forgive all of those people in the circle. Finally forgive yourself. Wrap yourself in light and love, and move on.

If you stop taking on other people's stuff, you won't have to do this activity again. You can be empathetic without baggage. Take care of you first, send loving-kindness to those who are struggling, but do NOT take on their shit. You have enough of your own and taking theirs is not your job.

Now, literally, return anything and everything you've ever borrowed. Books, CDs, Tupperware, clothes. Anything. This will further lighten your load and make more space for new good stuff to come in.

Day 28: Give People Their S@%* Back (figuratively and literally)

Questions to Ponder:

Whose shit have you been carrying around that you're ready to ditch?

_____
_____
_____
_____

What can you give away today to clean your slate?

_____
_____
_____
_____

Thought to Think:

I am releasing any thought or feeling that has been weighing me down.

Action to Take:

Clean out your closet, the trunk of your car, the junk drawer in your kitchen. Give unwanted clothes and shoes to Goodwill. Repeat over and over again, "Thank you. I love you," when you think of a thought or person that burdens you.

DAY 29
Control + Alt + Delete

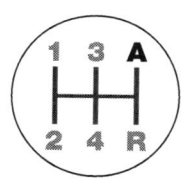

"Your sacred space is where you can find yourself again and again."

Joseph Campbell

Each person comes into the world a tabula rasa, and the moment we have our first thought as an itty-bitty baby, we separate ourselves from the great nothingness that is everything. We started as a blank piece of paper—empty of life experience, yet full of wisdom. As we live, each thought and experience adds a dot to our blank piece of paper, filling us up and taking us further and further away from who we really are.

Fully Engaged

There is no judgment in this. This process of filling up our space *is* the human experience, our own unique story that becomes our life. We lose ourselves in the dots and find ourselves in the spaces in between. These spaces are the moments of clarity and *aha* realizations that reset us back to who we were before we were all the dots.

We experience life in the dots (what the world *thinks* is real life) with little connection and meaning, only to realize that the more we get back to the clean slate, the more real we become. With less judgment and worry and fewer problems and blaming, the more connected we feel and the more purposeful life is. It isn't supposed to be a struggle. And it certainly doesn't have to be. You get to choose.

Humans struggle because we forget to hit Ctrl+Alt+Del to reboot ourselves back to our original state where something much bigger is in charge, not outside of us, but within us. Just as a computer that gets overworked and taxed by downloading and processing, we too take on too much in our lives, and we forget who we really are. It's time to reboot. It's time to erase some of the dots and get back to more blanks.

Day 29: Control + Alt + Delete

⏲ Questions to Ponder:

Where are you feeling stuck in the dots of your life?

_____
_____
_____
_____

When is the last time you had an aha moment, or a moment of clarity?

_____
_____
_____
_____

🔨 Thought to Think:

I am a blank slate, open and receptive to being who I really am.

⚙ Action to Take:

Get out a blank white sheet of paper. Look at it and realize this is who you started out as. Take a black magic marker and begin to make dots dispersed on the piece of paper. Continue making dots until your page is more black than white. Ask yourself where you can create space to live a more meaningful life.

Fully Engaged

Another beautiful way to reset yourself is through meditation. Set your timer for ten minutes and breathe, allowing your thoughts to drift by like clouds in the sky.

DAY 30

Stop Slouching! Stand Up and Be Proud to Be You!

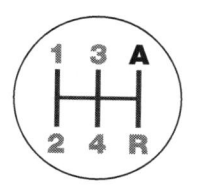

"Our bodies change our minds, and our minds can change our behavior, and our behavior can change our outcomes."

Amy Cuddy

As I walk around in the world, I notice a lot of people (including myself sometimes) shrinking, curling up, and generally acting small. Most of them are women.

Do a quick body audit now. How are you sitting? Would you consider your posture open or closed right now? Are you making yourself bigger or smaller?

Fully Engaged

When we slouch and constrict our bodies, we're consciously or subconsciously protecting ourselves from vulnerability, giving away our power to something or someone outside of us who otherwise shouldn't make us change how we feel. We are giving up our power to be who we really are.

A brilliant woman named Amy Cuddy conducted research that proves that our posture and how we display ourselves in the world contributes significantly to our success or lack thereof. She's done extensive research on "power poses." that shows when we act big with our body and our posture (think extending your arms out in victory after crossing the finish line), not only do others perceive us as more powerful, but chemical reactions occur in our bodies to *make us feel* more powerful. And when we *feel* more powerful, we *are* more powerful.

Cuddy is a Harvard Business School professor who wasn't even supposed to graduate from college, after being incapacitated in a car accident in her early twenties. She advocates that we should "Fake it until we become it."

Even if you don't feel powerful right now, practice making yourself bigger with your body. Push your shoulders up, back, and then down, allowing your heart to open up. Breathe deeply. (You've probably done something similar if you've done yoga.) Now open your arms out to your sides. Stand with your legs slightly spread. Ground yourself. Do

Day 30: Stop Slouching! Stand Up and Be Proud to Be You!

this for two minutes and there will be hormonal changes in your body that make you more powerful.

Questions to Ponder:

When do you feel powerful? Do you think your body shows it?

_____
_____
_____
_____

When do you feel small? Do you think your body shows it?

_____
_____
_____
_____

Thought to Think:

I am standing tall and I am proud and powerful!

Action to Take:

Watch Amy Cuddy's TED talk to learn more about this. You'll be glad you did! http://www.ted.com/talks/amy_cuddy_your_body_language_shapes_who_you_are.html

DAY 31

Everyone is Busy, So Stop Saying That!

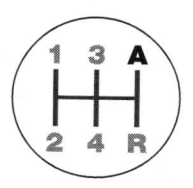

"Busy is a drug that a lot of people are addicted to."
Rob Bell

I recently saw a Facebook post that said "Stop the Glorification of Busy." Since when do we feel like we have to be sooooo busy to be cool? People who are overly busy tend to have ridiculously chaotic lives. And since chaotic lives are born in (or result in) chaotic minds, I am simply not interested. Nothing wonderful happens to people who are too busy to think freely and independently and creatively. Nothing serendipitous or intentional occurs when your page is entirely full of dots.

Fully Engaged

If you notice yourself saying you're "busy" every time someone asks you how you're doing, then this message is for YOU! Stop the glorification of busy. Press pause on your life for a moment and figure out where you can begin to say "no" and accept 80 percent instead of 100 percent. (Have you ever heard that before? If not: the idea is that if someone can do a particular thing 80 percent as well as you can, then you should delegate—that includes your husband doing the dishes and making the bed... but good luck, though, trying to foist those jobs on him.)

The bigger problem with being busy is thinking that our worth is born in busy, that if we don't have something to fill up every second of our day then we are somehow not worthy. This is why people fill their schedules up with useless meetings and things they are not truly invested in. Your worth is not in the number of appointments and meetings on your calendar. You're worthy because you're here. Let me repeat that. *You're worthy because you're here.* You don't have to *do* anything to prove yourself or to get others to notice you. Find peace in knowing that you deserve the very best life has to offer, even when you're relaxing on your sofa or knitting a scarf.

Put a halt to proving yourself. Stop the glorification of busy.

Day 31: Everyone is Busy, So Stop Saying That!

⏱ Questions to Ponder:

How full is your schedule? Where do you need to say no, or delegate?

_____
_____
_____
_____

When is the last time you told someone you were busy? How often do you do that?

_____
_____
_____
_____

🪨 Thought to Think:

I am worthy because I AM.

⚙ Action to Take:

Read this blog post about how we tie our worthiness to busy-ness: http://www.positivelypositive.com/2013/01/05/are-you-sooo-busy/

Sit on the couch for five minutes and practice not being busy. (Do NOT turn on the TV!)

DAY 32

Tame is (Mostly) Lame

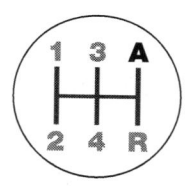

"You were once wild here. Don't let them tame you."
Isadora Duncan

We have been taught to ride the middle line, to play it safe and—by all means! —to NOT stand out. We have tamed ourselves to the point of being lame. This makes us think and act like the masses and if you've watched the news lately or taken a good look around while shopping at a mall, you realize this might not be the best thing.

Because we haven't been encouraged through our environment and surroundings to be who we are, we follow the crowd and do what we're "supposed" to. A humdrum life ensues, courtesy of the Henry Ford effect.

Fully Engaged

The perfect example of this is the classrooms we were brought up in, where we all sat in nice orderly rows following what the teacher said, doing our best not to ruffle any feathers. (Well, some of us did that). It takes guts to stand out. It takes guts to be you.

I sometimes ask in my talks, "Who in the audience was a troublemaker in school?" Inevitably, a few hands go up. Often if I have the opportunity to speak with these people afterwards, they tend to be the entrepreneurs and free thinkers who have the most interesting lives.

Have you ever heard the saying, "Well-behaved women rarely make history?" I have a love/hate relationship with that one. In some regards I believe that's true. And in others, I think that we can be well-behaved AND be ourselves. But society has encouraged us to believe this is not possible, that to be awesome you have to be a gun-slinging, Annie Oakley-type rebel. I don't think it's one extreme or the other. I think you can be kind and be yourself. I think you can care about people and be awesomely unique and untamed. So, let's change the stereotype. Let's teach the world that you can be tender-hearted and still be a badass.

Day 32: Tame is (Mostly) Lame

Questions to Ponder:

What do you do to blend in and appear tame?

_____
_____
_____
_____

What can you do today to just be you?

_____
_____
_____
_____

Thought to Think:

I am done with being tame (and lame).

Action to Take:

Notice the tame(lame)ness of conformity at work or on the subway today. Notice people being themselves. Be yourself and support others who are being themselves today, without judgment. Watch your mind in the process. And be kind.

DAY 33
Misery is Optional

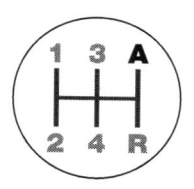

> *"Pain is inevitable. Suffering is optional."*
> **Haruki Murakami**

Yes, shitty things will happen to you (if you haven't figured that out already), but misery is still optional. I remember this when I'm throwing myself a massive pity party because I don't feel or look my best. Most of us have automatic negative thoughts (also known as ANTS). And I'll be the first person to tell you that I do. (Why do you think I'm writing this book?)

I have (am recovering from) the terrible habit of thinking the worst in many situations (remember those *Worst Case Scenario* books?), and you likely have too. My sister told me the other day that it's called "catastrophizing." Yep, that would be it. It's our cultural default. To change this you have to change the misery habit loop in your head. Our brains are wired to notice threat. This was helpful when there were saber-toothed tigers running around, but not so much now.

This is how the misery habit loop goes: something unpleasant happens (you have to pee REALLY bad and can't get up on the plane) and your mind kicks into primitive survival mode (also known as the amygdala hijack) and starts thinking of the worst possible thing that can happen (you piss yourself), and then the negative thought snowball keeps building momentum and rolling faster. (No, this hasn't happened to *me* lately. LOL.) You start to sweat, you start to think of all the negative "what ifs" of that worst case scenario. In the long run, the seatbelt light is turned off and you're permitted to go relieve yourself.

So what should you do instead? When you get in an uncomfortable situation, breathe and remember that "this too shall pass." A few minutes of discomfort are insignificant in the grand scale of life. Be compassionate with yourself instead of being annoyed about your situation. Say kind things in your self-talk.

It's unrealistic to think these unpleasant things will not happen to you. They will. Every day. It's all about how you

Day 33: Misery is Optional

handle them and comfort yourself. I sometimes say to myself "disconnect," because I know that by staying connected to the drama of my thoughts, I'm going to end up somewhere I don't want to be.

Questions to Ponder:

What are your misery triggers?

_____
_____
_____
_____

What can you practice to calm yourself when you're having a bad moment?

_____
_____
_____
_____

Thought to Think:

I am able to manage whatever comes my way. This too shall pass.

Fully Engaged

⚙️ Action to Take:

Spend the next week noticing your triggers. (For example, one of mine is being in airports.) What situations are you in where you feel uncomfortable? Write them all down and think of a positive action or thought you can take when you're in those situations to erase the misery habit loop.

DAY 34
Too Big for Your Britches

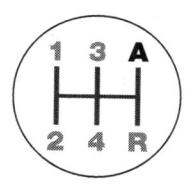

> "The great mass of human beings are not acutely selfish. After the age of about thirty they abandon individual ambition—in many cases, indeed, they almost abandon the sense of being individuals at all—and live chiefly for others, or are simply smothered under drudgery."
>
> **George Orwell**

"Don't get too big for your britches," my mom would say. (And if you don't know, that has nothing to do with gaining weight. It's simply a good ole Southern way of warning against becoming conceited.)

Fully Engaged

In our culture, we learn that to stand out = selfishness. Of course there are a few examples of people who stand out and are unapologetically themselves (think Madonna or Lady Gaga), but they are somehow "different" from us. "They" are the people we look at and admire, while saying we could never be anything like them. "They," for whatever reason, are of a whole different kind and mind. "We" must stay in our little boxes and remain in britches of the proper size.

Who are we to think we deserve to stand out? It is engrained from childhood that the best way to be loved and gain the approval of others is to blend in. We are taught this at the schoolhouse and at home. But where's the creativity, people? We teach people how to fit in. Yes, there is some value in learning to do certain things to maintain a general lifestyle, but all too often we become constant chameleons, changing colors with our surroundings, forgetting who we are and ignoring our potential.

In fact, just the other day on *The X Factor*, a contestant said that one reason she felt she could win was because she was a chameleon. Argh. She didn't win. The world doesn't want chameleons. We want people who are unapologetically themselves.

I also notice this in regard to how people dress. I prefer to wear bright colors and funky things (e.g., sparkly red TOMS and a bright cobalt Furla purse!). And when I do, I have to

Day 34: Too Big for Your Britches

be prepared because people will call it out. Because I'm not in the uniform gray and black, I stand out and I have to be ok with that. If I were self-conscious about it, I'd stick with the uniform. I do have a lot of gray and black—but I always throw in a pop of color somewhere.

It's ok to be really talented at something. It's ok to stand out. It's awesome to know and use your strengths. It's fantastic to be a leader. It's good to be yourself.

Questions to Ponder:

On a scale of 1 to 10, 10 being the highest, how comfortable are you with standing out?

_____
_____
_____

When is the last time you did something you were proud of? What was it?

_____
_____
_____

Fully Engaged

Thought to Think:

I am proud to stand out because I'm awesome!

Action to Take:

Bust the button on your britches today. Be proud of who you are and what you've accomplished. Tell somebody about it even if it feels like you're bragging. Spend as much time today as possible being too big for your britches and see what it feels like, because chances are you've never done it before. Add a pop of color (a scarf, some fun shoes or jewelry) to your outfit today.

DAY 35

The Habit of Living on the Surface

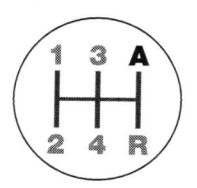

"People who cannot invent and reinvent themselves must be content with borrowed postures, secondhand ideas, fitting in instead of standing out."

Warren Bennis

Much of life is spent on the surface, skimming the top, staying safe where we know we won't get in trouble, offend anyone, or risk not knowing all the facts. But the surface is rocky. The surface is where all the waves are. We get knocked around a lot when we stay on the surface.

We stick to the surface life because it gets us what we want—insta-love, acceptance, and approval from the crowd. We

Fully Engaged

learn the habit as children. When we're children, throwing a tantrum or showing our true colors in a way that our parents, loved ones, teachers and friends deem "inappropriate" gets us punished, put in the corner, ousted for showing emotion and being real. After a few hits, it's easier to give up and fit in. We say to ourselves, "Yes, the world may be able handle me in small doses, but being me full-time is too much work. I am free to shine in solitude, but maybe too bright for the masses. With the masses, I am safe. Without them, I am alone." As children, vulnerable does not feel good. In fact it feels downright scary! The surface life often persists when we are adults. We have light conversations, we watch reality TV, we talk about the weather, blah blah blah, all the while getting smacked in the face with wave after wave of the mediocre life.

The habit of living on the surface has caused us to forget who we are and makes us anxious. Getting knocked around by waves beats up on you after a while. Diving below the surface where it's less crowded allows you to slow down and BE. It allows you to be still and receptive to something new and brilliant. Activities (or non-activities) like yoga, meditation, or anything where you get "in the flow" and lose track of time, take you to that deep well of wisdom within.

Day 35: The Habit of Living on the Surface

Questions to Ponder:

What do you think about visiting the depths of your soul more often?

_____
_____
_____
_____

What might you find out about yourself if you go there?

_____
_____
_____
_____

Thought to Think:

I am moving beyond the surface life and finding out who I really am.

Action to Take:

Set a timer and sit and breathe for ten minutes. Allow the thoughts to come and go like clouds passing in the sky. Turn off your TV for the day. Pay deep attention and be present all day.

DAY 36
Go for It!

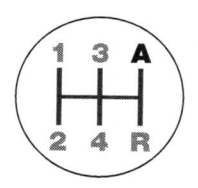

"If you're offered a seat on a rocket ship, you don't ask what seat. You just get on."

Sheryl Sandberg

We often spend way too much time getting ready. We think that the more we prepare and consider every detail, the more successful we'll be. That's not always true. Sometimes the preparation portion of the journey takes WAAAAAYYYYY too long, and we look down after five years and realize that we still haven't started on that thing that we really wanted to accomplish. Don't allow the preparation to become the journey. I'm giving you permission to stop planning and get at it.

Fully Engaged

You are ready…

    … to make a change
    … to be happy for no reason at all
    … to do something bigger than you've ever done
    … to be the person you've always wanted to be
    … to travel the world
    … to make new friends
    … to start all over again
    … to learn a new language
    … to get a new wardrobe
    … to change your look
    … to give more time to yourself
    … to be more (or less) empathetic to others
    … to change your eating and exercise habits
    … to break free from your past
    … to play a new sport
    … to get a new haircut
    … to change jobs
    … to stop settling
    … to reinvent yourself
    … to be your happiest and best self
    … to live a meaningful life
    … _____
    … _____
    … _____

Day 36: Go for It!

Questions to Ponder:

What are you prepared to do that you haven't done yet?

_____
_____
_____
_____

What are you waiting for?

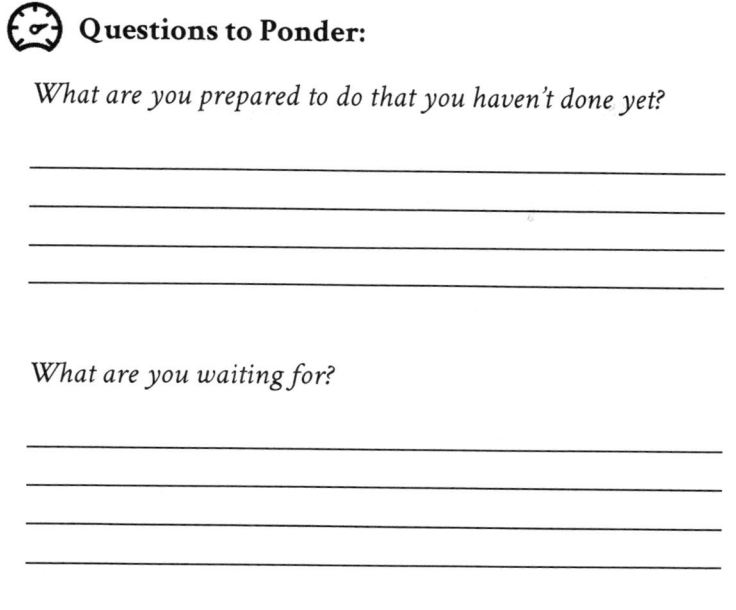

_____
_____
_____
_____

Thought to Think:

I am ready to do something I've always wanted to do.

Action to Take:

Fill in the blanks above and stop pussy-footing around. This is your life! Go live it.

DAY 37
Clarity = Power

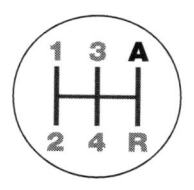

"It's a lack of clarity that creates chaos and frustration. Those emotions are poison to any living goal."
Dr. Steve Maraboli

Though math is not my forté, I adopted this simple equation as the foundation of my personal truth ever since I heard it at an empowerment training years ago. Perhaps it's my "who, what, when, where" journalistic background, or my slightly type-A personality that demands clarity. But whatever it is, I accept it as a personal truth and one of my highest values because clarity has equated to more power in my own life experience.

Fully Engaged

Whether it's one of my biggest life goals or my most menial daily tasks, I stop to ask myself, "What do I really, really want?" as often as I remember. (Sing Spice Girls song here.) When I align my intention with the action I choose, I move forward with a better grip on what to expect and often get exactly what I intend.

Our personal power is our ability to create our lives for the highest benefit of ourselves and all involved. If we are unclear about what we want, we give our power away to the circumstances, people, and events that surround us. Stand firm in your power by being clear in your communication, clear in your direction, clear in your purpose, clear in your intent. And don't worry. You can be flexible too. If you change your mind, simply change your intention.

I'm clear that I'm not a mathematician, but I do know something about proportions: our level of clarity is directly related to our level of personal power. More clarity = More power.

Be clear. Be powerful.

Day 37: Clarity = Power

Questions to Ponder:

How clear are you with yourself and others?

___

Where can you be clearer in your life?

___

Thought to Think:

I am clear and powerful.

Action to Take:

As you approach every situation today, ask yourself, "What do I really, really want from this?" To take this even further, list your goals (one year, five years, ten years) and then align your life around those, making sure that your moments are purposeful and meaningful.

Fully Engaged

Read and participate in my first book, Live with Intention: 10 Steps to Creating the Life of Your Dreams. And watch this Spice Girls video: https://www.youtube.com/watch?v=gJLIiF15wjQ.

You'll be glad you did!

DAY 38

Your Ten Objects

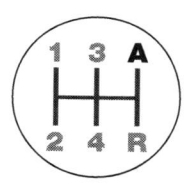

"The aim of art is to represent not the outward appearance of things, but their inward significance."
Aristotle

I recently read an article written by a life coach who gets her clients to bring ten articles that best represent their values/loves/life-joys to their first session together. I loved the idea and this morning gathered the articles I feel best represent me.

Journal = I love to write, reflect, and constantly grow. I find peace and harmony in the process of journaling.

Fully Engaged

Running shoes = I enjoy my commitment to running and finding "my happy pace." It's cathartic and healing and as my mother said, as a child, I ran before I walked.

Castanets = I dance to the rhythm of life, I'm fluent in Spanish, and I love to travel.

Inspirational card deck = I'm always looking on the bright side of things and learning more about myself. These help me reflect and stay upbeat.

Fresh flowers = I love having vases of fresh flowers all over our house. They make me feel alive and remind me of the cycle of life.

iPhone = It's important for me to connect authentically with others through texts, phone calls, emails and Facebook. I also love listening to music on my iPhone, and using it to track my runs.

Passport = I love to travel because I feel present in new places. I love meeting new people and learning new things that only travel can teach. (And I read this article by the life coach I'm talking about in a British magazine called *Red* as I was flying home from London.)

Day 38: Your Ten Objects

Banana = I eat at least one every day. It represents my commitment to healthful eating and the "monkey mind" that I do my best to tame as often as possible.

Buddha = I enjoy the quiet and stillness of meditation and yoga and appreciate remembering the God-being that I am through non-activities. This statue is a reminder. It sits on a shelf by my bed.

Microphone = I believe I was put on this planet to teach, inspire and empower. The microphone reminds me of my strong voice and my purpose.

Questions to Ponder:

What ten objects best represent you?

_____
_____
_____
_____

How do your values align with the objects?

_____
_____
_____
_____

Fully Engaged

Action to Take:

Gather up your ten objects. Take a photo of them. Put it on Instagram with #tenobjects and @adaircates.

DAY 39

What Do You Value?

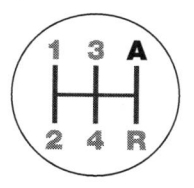

"*Money is the barometer of a society's virtue.*"

Ayn Rand

In gathering all the necessary documents for my taxes, I took the opportunity to go through my credit card and bank statements to see what expenses I had accrued during the year. It made me remember that I spend money (and time) on the things that I value. The statements make it clear that I love to eat out and travel (and shop at Target and J. Crew). While that's true, I want to balance that spending with more intentional saving for rainy days, larger items, and my later years. (I have to reign in my impulsive, instant gratification self sometimes. It's a tough practice and I will love myself in the process.)

Fully Engaged

While this may seem like not that big of a deal, these things and experiences we value amount to our life. Every single decision we make becomes part of our overall life picture and story. We are creating our life each time we spend money or time. Now, don't go overboard on this to the point of paralysis. Remember, we are imperfect human creatures doing the best we can. Be mindful AND be gentle when you mess up, and pay attention to where your attention goes. Energy flows where attention goes.

Questions to Ponder:

Where do you spend your money?

_____
_____
_____
_____

Where do you spend your time?

_____
_____
_____
_____

Day 39: What Do You Value?

Thought to Think:

I spend my money and time intentionally.

Action to Take:

Pull out your credit card or bank statement from last month. Make a list of the top five places you spent money. Do they align with your values?

To keep track of where you spend your time, spend one week writing down what you did all day and how much time you spent doing it. It's an amazing awareness that will certainly be an impetus for change (if you choose to change anything).

Monday _____
Tuesday _____
Wednesday _____
Thursday _____
Friday _____
Saturday _____
Sunday _____

DAY 40
My Personal Credo

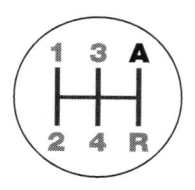

"Go put your creed into the deed nor speak with double tongue."

Ralph Waldo Emerson

I share this credo in hopes that you will consider the truths that govern your life. How we see the world is how we experience the world.

1. I always have the power to choose my thoughts and to choose how I respond to circumstances, people and events.
2. The best circumstances, people and events surface when I don't get too emotionally trapped or attached to the outcome, when I give things some time and

space to work themselves out. My best creations have been the easiest to start but the hardest to finish.
3. When I get happy right where I am, opportunities to increase my happiness present themselves even more.
4. I know the difference between an action that feels forced and an action that feels inspired. I am better at inspired action.
5. I can have what I want if I am willing to see it and accept it and be disciplined enough to take steady action towards it.
6. Distractions may present themselves on my way to reaching my goals, and giving them attention only takes that energy away from my goal.
7. I am never stuck. The world is never standing still.
8. Amazing things present themselves at just the right time when I'm clear and feeling good.
9. I am a strong woman and a powerful creator. I am excited about what's in store for me.
10. No matter where I am or who I am with or what I am doing, misery is optional! Sometimes I choose misery, but most of the time I don't. The moments of misery remind me that life is too short to *not* be happy.
11. Some days are going to suck. My mantra when that happens: This too shall pass, and I shall learn from it.

Day 40: My Personal Credo

Questions to Ponder:

Which of the 11 credos resonated most with you?

_____
_____
_____
_____

What thoughts came up for you as you read through these?

_____
_____
_____
_____

Thought to Think:

I am living my credo.

Action to Take:

Start writing your own credo. You can have any number of statements and don't have to write them all in one sitting. In fact, it's better if you put down your feelings and allow them to gradually morph over time.

DAY 41

Bark with Passion!

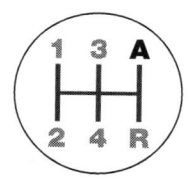

"The most courageous act is still to think for yourself. Aloud."

Coco Chanel

My dog Mozart barks with passion much in the same way as I imagine the real Mozart composed his classical hits. We've tried special collars and positive (and not-so-positive) reinforcement to make him stop, but when he's in police mode, watch out! He is gonna bark at the top of his lungs, stopping only long enough to snort to catch his breath. It drives me bat-shit crazy, but it reminds me that when I have something to say, I need to say it. Unlike Mozart, I can filter opportunities to bark or not. If I bark all the time, after a while no one will listen anymore. If I never

Fully Engaged

bark, I'm repressing all of my opinions, and they will show up at a later date as anger or maybe even cancer.

I had an opportunity to bark (with passion!) recently when my dogs and I almost got run over in a pedestrian crosswalk. Instinct kicked in and I looked that crazy driver in the eyes and screamed some choice profanities. Weird experience for someone who doesn't experience anger much—but it made me realize that I stuff those emotions down a lot, keep them under control to appear calm, cool and collected until my "fight or flight" mentality gets triggered. Apparently I went into "fight" mode.

There's a bumper sticker out there that says "Wag more. Bark less." I like that bumper sticker because people should be happier! Wagging is wonderful and necessary on your journey to living your meaningful life, and when you feel passionate about something, SEIZE the opportunity to speak up. Bark on!

Day 41: Bark with Passion!

⊙ Questions to Ponder:

When have you not seized an opportunity to speak up and regretted it?

_____
_____
_____
_____

What's the perfect balance of barking and wagging for you?

_____
_____
_____
_____

◼ Thought to Think:

I am balanced at barking and wagging.

⚙ Action to Take:

Try barking today (without biting). Instead of holding your tongue, speak up, go first and tell 'em how you really feel.

DAY 42

Falling in Love with ME!

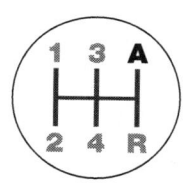

"You must love yourself before you love another. By accepting yourself and fully being what you are, your simple presence can make others happy. You yourself, as much as anybody in the entire universe, deserve your love and affection."

Buddha

Today I made a commitment to fall in love with myself all over again, to recognize the unique awesome sauce that I bring into the world and to be proud of who I am.

Those of you who know me may think I'm confident and self-assured, because outwardly I am. But you don't know how damn mean I can be to myself in my head, saying things

Fully Engaged

I wouldn't dare say to someone else. In fact, my problem is, I'm nicer to others than I am to myself, which sets up an incongruence in my being that makes me feel anxious and misaligned. *Yuck.*

My new commitment started at 7:27 this morning when I wrote this in my journal: "I'm allowing myself to be kinder to myself and have courage, compassion, and connection. It truly is a journey to own my vulnerability (thank you, Brené Brown!) and my moments of shame and recognize them while being kind to myself. I am aware of how I talk to myself—and especially in moments of not feeling my best, I'm a real asshole. Instead of getting irritated and wishing things would be other than they are (what I normally do), I'm going to imagine what I'd say to my best friend or a small child who was having the same kinds of thoughts. I uplift and encourage myself and then just allow the discomfort. Breathing into it. I want this to be a new way of living for me—not just a passing trend. Practicing compassion for me first. Pep-talking myself through the day, if that's what it takes. Disconnecting from automatic negative thoughts (ANTS) and connecting with something bigger than me. Letting go of perfectionism and embracing what is. Not getting mad when things aren't perfect—just allowing. Doing my best to feel good but being compassionate with myself when I'm not. I am worthy. I deserve the best and accept the best right now. My thoughts to myself can be

Day 42: Falling in Love with ME!

so cruel. I am deserving and worthy of being positive and uplifting to me."

This is a process and not something to get all perfectionistic about. Day by day and moment by moment, asking myself, "How can I be kind to myself right now?"

I had to come back to this intention and to my journal this afternoon because I noticed that my day turned out so differently from what I expected. First, I had a great day at the office, for the first time in a long time. Then, I got an inquiry to speak at an event on the topic of "philanthropy and women in power" (yay!). My day ended with my boss calling me to schedule some time to discuss and document evidence to send to HR that I deserve a salary increase. I wonder how much more wonderful-ness life will reveal to me as I learn to love myself more and more?

😊 Questions to Ponder:

How do you talk to yourself?

_____
_____
_____
_____

Fully Engaged

What can you do to make a commitment to being nicer to yourself?

_____
_____
_____
_____

Thought to Think:

I am loving myself more and more every day.

Action to Take:

Make a written commitment to yourself to fall in love with you all over again. When you're feeling down, be gentle on yourself, and give yourself a pep talk when you need it. Treat yourself as you would your dearest friend or a small child you adore.

And most importantly, read something by Brené Brown. She changed my life and will likely change yours too!

DAY 43

Be Willing to Receive

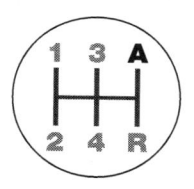

"Make sure you don't go to the ocean with a teaspoon. At least take a bucket so the kids won't laugh at you."
Jim Rohn

Sometimes the hardest part of giving is receiving. When someone gives you a compliment, don't automatically give a compliment back. Receive the compliment and say, "thank you," and move on. When you automatically give the compliment back, you rob the other person of the opportunity to purely give, and that never feels good. It may take some practice to get this one down, but once you become more accustomed to receiving, everyone will feel better. And once you love yourself more, you'll see that you truly deserve it.

Fully Engaged

I recently took a trip to Nashville and had the opportunity to see this in action. If you've ever been there, you know there are buskers and bands of all shapes, sizes and smells on Broadway—soloist female artists covering Janis Joplin, country wanna-bes singing Clint Black, duos and groups, sitting and standing, strumming and drumming, sober and not-so-much.

With their multitude of nuances, they all have one thing in common: a tip jar. Most people use a fishbowl or a gas can; however, one talented group of hillbilly country artists (who were certainly unafraid to receive) had a giant wash bucket and it was FULL of cash. I saw them on the strip three different times and each time they had a huge crowd and a wash bucket of cash, while the other musicians had a few coins and dollars to boast about. Yes, they were good and had a great energy mojo, but they also had a bigger bucket open and ready to receive. The bigger the tip jar, the bigger the tip. The more willing you are to receive, the more you will receive.

Day 43: Be Willing to Receive

🕹 Questions to Ponder:

How do you respond when someone gives you a compliment?

_____
_____
_____
_____

How big is your tip jar?

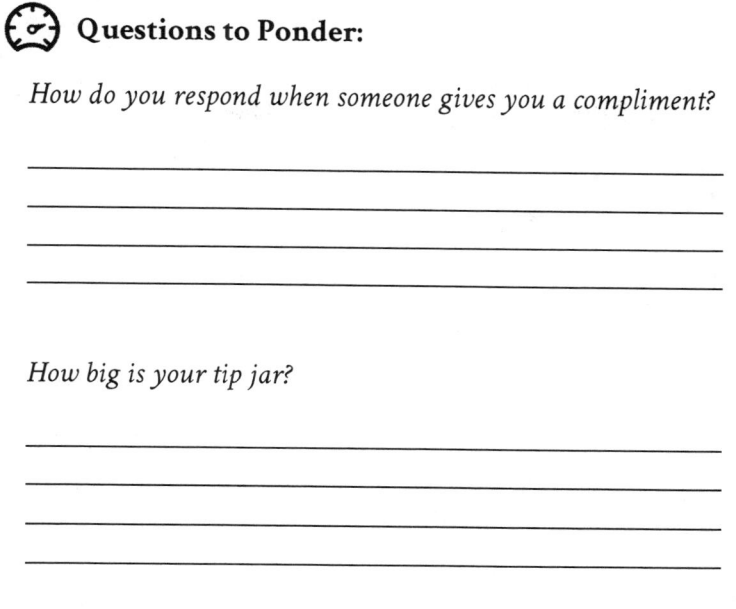

_____
_____
_____
_____

🛢 Thought to Think:

I am open and willing and ready to receive more good in my life.

⚙ Action to Take:

For a whole week, practice the art of receiving. Initially, don't concern yourself with what you're giving back. Say thank you when you get a compliment (and that's all) —and get a bigger bucket, for goodness sakes!

DAY 44

Practice DOES NOT Makes Perfect

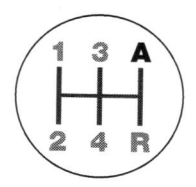

"It is common sense to take a method and try it. If it fails, admit it frankly and try another. But above all, try something."

Franklin Delano Roosevelt

Were you told as a child that "practice makes perfect"? (I was.) Obviously, if we practice something we'll get better at it, but expecting perfection is setting ourselves up for failure. What if instead of practicing for perfection, we just practiced? Practiced getting better every day, being kinder to ourselves and others, being vulnerable, admitting our mistakes, accepting our shortcomings? Wouldn't that make for a more joyful and meaningful life?

Fully Engaged

This is the overarching philosophy of yoga: show up to your mat and do the best you can. Some days you will be able to touch your toes and some days you won't. That's ok. At least you show up. At least you practice.

I often got "in trouble" for making careless mistakes as a child (aka practicing). I would rush through a test (most likely because I was bored stiff), misread something, and choose the wrong answer.

These silly little careless mistakes are long in my past. But I wonder if I had completely latched onto this idea and said to myself, "I make careless mistakes" that I would have totally paralyzed myself into perfectionism? Well, maybe I have done that a little bit. Ugh. I'm a fast learner and I move at a rapid pace, so yes, along the way I make mistakes. But who cares? At least I'm going for it. I am practicing perfectly imperfect from now on and remembering that practice is better than perfect!

Day 44: Practice DOES NOT Makes Perfect

Questions to Ponder:

How often do you NOT do something because you know you won't be immediately good at it?

_____
_____
_____
_____

What can you practice today to feel better?

_____
_____
_____
_____

Thought to Think:

I am practicing imperfection.

Action to Take:

Go take a yoga class and give yourself a pat on the back for showing up to the mat. Carry that philosophy over to other areas of your life.

DAY 45
Growth Can Be Uncomfortable

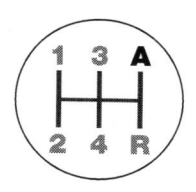

"And the day came when the risk to remain tight in a bud was more painful than the risk it took to blossom."
Anais Nin

We tend to move towards things that bring us pleasure and away from things that bring us pain, yet the things that bring us temporary "pain" are often just what we need to go through to live a fully engaged life. Being uncomfortable is often the first step in learning and growing. So, if you want your life to stay exactly as it is now, then avoid pain. If you want something new, you're going to have to risk being uncomfortable, at least for a little while. Most people are so afraid of discomfort that they completely miss amazing opportunities for change that will improve their lives in ways they never thought possible.

Though I can't say that I love being uncomfortable (who does?), I will give myself a pat on the back because I am pretty good at allowing myself to feel discomfort—I've done it enough to see the rewards. One of the most uncomfortable times in my life was when I lived in Spain during college and had to learn a whole new language. I was good at Spanish in high school, but this was a whole new ballgame. The woman I lived with spoke no English, and neither did most of the people I interacted with on a daily basis. As a person who loves to talk and someone who was WAY consumed with being perfect, this was a challenging journey full of many moments of silence and awkwardness. My ability to speak Spanish is still with me today because I endured those difficult moments. In fact, I think the vulnerability I experienced had a lot to do with shaping me into the person I am today.

Day 45: Growth Can Be Uncomfortable

Questions to Ponder:

What discomfort are you avoiding?

___

What would it look like to experience and move through that discomfort?

___

Thought to Think:

I am easily and effortlessly moving through discomfort and into a more meaningful life.

Action to Take:

Intentionally choose something today that is uncomfortable. Not something to torture yourself just for the sake of it, but something you've always wanted to try. Paint a canvas, sign up for voice lessons, dust off your Rosetta Stone.

DAY 46

This Is Going to Sound Morbid, But Don't Skip This!

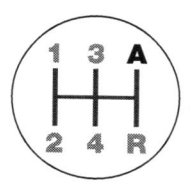

*"Of all the words of mice and men, the saddest are,
'It might have been.'"*

Kurt Vonnegut

Reading *The Top Five Regrets of the Dying* by Bronnie Ware made me realize that THIS IS EXACTLY WHY I'M WRITING THIS BOOK! My passion and purpose in life are to inspire others to live a life of meaning so they don't get to their final days of life with these same regrets. Bronnie Ware, a palliative care nurse who began asking those she cared for in their last days of life what their deepest regrets were, came up with this list. If you want to read more, I suggest you purchase her book. For now, read them and ponder:

Fully Engaged

> *I wish I'd had the courage to live a life true to myself, not the life others expected of me.*
>
> *I wish I hadn't worked so hard.*
>
> *I wish I'd had the courage to express my feelings.*
>
> *I wish I had stayed in touch with my friends.*
>
> *I wish that I had let myself be happier.*

This list makes me sad. I don't ever want anyone to feel this way at the end of his/her life. The good news is, you're still alive. If any of these regrets weigh on you, this is your opportunity to consciously decide to make a change.

Questions to Ponder:

Which one of the regrets resonates most with you? Why?

_____
_____
_____
_____

Day 46: This Is Going to Sound Morbid, But Don't Skip This!

What do you think you could change about your life to let that one go?

_____
_____
_____
_____

Thought to Think:

I am living a full and happy life of no regrets.

Action to Take:

Read a brief article about the five regrets here: http://myscienceacademy.org/2013/05/14/the-top-5-regrets-of-the-dying/

Talk to the eldest living member of your family and ask him/her what he/she most regrets about life and what they'd do differently. Take note and make the necessary changes. Life is too short for regrets!

Conclusion

"To be sure, man's search for meaning may arouse inner tension rather than inner equilibrium. However, precisely such tension is an indispensable prerequisite of mental health. There is nothing in the world, I venture to say, that would so effectively help one survive even the worst conditions as the knowledge that there is a meaning in one's life."
Viktor Frankl

I hope you've enjoyed the journey of the last forty-six days. What have you learned? What are your takeaways? And most importantly, what now? (Feel free to consider these questions in your journal.) I hope these days truly feel like "the first days of the rest of your life," and that you want to continue along the new paths you've forged for yourself.

Though man's search for meaning has been eternal, it also feels as though these last several years of coming through a recession and the new generation of Millennials moving into the workplace are helping us transition into a world of living a more fully engaged in life. (Want to learn more? Read this: http://www.nytimes.com/2013/12/01/opinion/sunday/millennial-searchers.html?_r=0).

You taking the time to work through this book and ponder some deep-thought questions and act in new ways has facilitated that shift. Imagine how different the world would be if people let go of superficial thinking and small talk, and shifted to deeper and more significant conversations. Now that you've had this experience, I encourage you to share it with others. Use the questions in the book as table topics at your next social event, post the quotes on Facebook or Instagram, and stay in touch with me on your journey.

Meaning and fulfillment are inside of you no matter what's happening in the outside world. It's up to YOU to be well and fulfilled, vivacious and happy. The world is not going to do it for you (and will sometimes do everything it can to throw you off your path). And to get away from "normal," you have to go kicking and screaming in the opposite direction, shaking off status quo as if you're fleeing a beehive.

You don't want to end up on your deathbed like Leo Tolstoy's character Ivan Ilyich:

> *It was true, as the doctor said, that Ivan Ilyich's physical sufferings were terrible, but worse than the physical sufferings were his mental sufferings which were his chief torture.*

Conclusion

His mental sufferings were due to the fact that that night, as he looked at Gerasim's sleepy, good-natured face with its prominent cheek bones, the question suddenly occurred to him: "What if my whole life has been wrong?"

It occurred to him that what had appeared perfectly impossible before, namely that he had not spent his life as he should have done, might after all be true. It occurred to him that his scarcely perceptible attempts to struggle against what was considered good by the most highly placed people, those scarcely noticeable impulses which he had immediately suppressed, might have been the real thing, and all the rest false. And his professional duties and the whole arrangement of his life and of his family, and all his social and official interests, might all have been false. He tried to defend all those things to himself and suddenly felt the weakness of what he was defending. There was nothing to defend.

This book was first published in 1866. And almost 150 years later, here we are pondering the same questions. There is no grander pursuit than living the purpose of your life. You've started the journey of a thousand miles. I wish you well and encourage you to be the best that you can be. Enjoy the rest of the journey!

Made in the USA
Charleston, SC
03 June 2015